rEVELATIONS

James Harpur

Elizabeth Hallam, Consultant

rEVELATIONS
The mEDIEVAL *World*

A HENRY HOLT REFERENCE BOOK

HENRY HOLT AND COMPANY

NEW YORK

A Henry Holt Reference Book
Henry Holt and Company, Inc.
Publishers since 1866
115 West 18th Street
New York, New York 10011

Henry Holt® is a registered trademark of
Henry Holt and Company, Inc.

Library of Congress Cataloging-in-Publication Data
Revelations, the Medieval world / James Harpur;
Elizabeth Hallam, consultant. — 1st ed.
p.   cm. — (Henry Holt reference book)
Includes bibliographical references and index.
1. Middle Ages—History.   I. Hallam, Elizabeth M.
II. Title.   III. Series.
D117.H28   1995   95-970
909.07—dc20   CIP
ISBN 0-8050-4140-0

Henry Holt books are available for special
promotions and premiums.
For details contact: Director, Special Markets.

First Edition—1995

Edited and designed by
Marshall Editions, London

Concept: Katherine Harkness
Editor: James Bremner
Art editor: Katherine Harkness
Picture editor: Elizabeth Loving
Assistant editor: Simon Beecroft

Originated by Fotographics
Printed and bound in Italy by Officine Grafiche
De Agostini – Novara

All first editions are printed on acid-free paper. ∞

10 9 8 7 6 5 4 3 2 1

C O

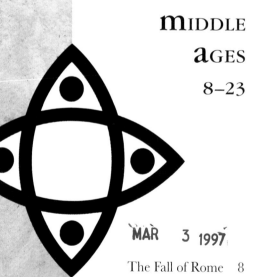

MAR   3 1997

NTENTS

FOREWORD

When in 1095 the First Crusade was launched by Pope Urban II, it was said of the Crusaders that "They carry weapons of war, they wear the cross of Christ on their right shoulder or back, and with one voice they cry out: 'God wills it, God wills it, God wills it.'"

Two dominant characteristics of the Middle Ages are here given vivid expression. The first is piety, to which numerous costly and magnificent cathedrals and churches, ornamented with stained glass, sculptures, mosaics, and frescoes, still attest. The second is pugnacity: whether driven by faith, love of adventure, or greed, warfare was endemic in medieval Europe. It produced castles, weaponry both ingenious and crude, and a code of chivalry honored as much in the breach as in the observance.

In *Revelations: The Medieval World*, key themes – kings and castles, town and country, cathedrals and churches, monks and monasteries, and the arts of warfare – are interwoven to provide a lively and authoritative introduction to the medieval period in western Europe from about 1000 to 1500. Five gatefolds corresponding to the themes form the focus and bring the Middle Ages alive in a fresh, distinctive, and original way.

The book also reveals a continuity of human experience which cuts across the centuries and the cultural contrasts dividing us from our medieval ancestors. For medieval nobles and peasants, as for us, the world was not only beset with warfare, but also with climatic disasters and epidemics. Nor have human emotions changed. For example, the French abbess Heloise's recollections of her youthful relationship with her lover, the charismatic scholar and teacher Peter Abelard, still have a freshness and immediacy that is timeless: "When you appeared in public, who did not rush to catch a glimpse of you... Every young girl was on fire in your presence... But it was desire, not affection, which bound you to me, the flame of lust rather than love...."

Elizabeth Hallam

Elizabeth Hallam

W HEN THE BRIGHTEST LIGHT WAS extinguished, when the whole world perished in one city, then I was dumb with silence." So wrote Saint Jerome, a noted scholar living in monastic seclusion in Bethlehem, on hearing that Rome had been sacked by the Germanic tribe of the Visigoths in 410. Although the physical destruction was not great and the Goths later moved off to invade Gaul, the psychological repercussions were profound, since Rome's almost mythic inviolability had been shown to be a chimera.

The sacking of Rome was one of the more significant events that marked the long decline and eventual fall of the Roman Empire. But as Germanic barbarian tribes increasingly conquered areas of the empire, the fusion of their tribal customs with surviving Roman institutions, culture, and language helped to create the characteristics that became typical of the medieval period.

The reason for the demise of Rome has been one of the most debated of all historical questions. Moral laxity; the pacifist tendencies of Christianity, which was made the state religion in the fourth century; excessive taxation and social discontent; economic stagnation; epidemics and climatic conditions – all have been put forward as possible factors. Whatever the underlying reasons, however, the immediate cause was the invasion of Germanic tribes in the fifth century A.D.

At the start of the previous century, the idea of the empire's disintegration must have seemed an unlikely prospect to contemporaries. In 312, Constantine the Great, inspired by a vision of the Christian cross, defeated a rival to become emperor of the western half of the Roman Empire – which had previously been divided into two by Emperor Diocletian (284–305). In 324, Constantine defeated Licinius, the eastern emperor, and

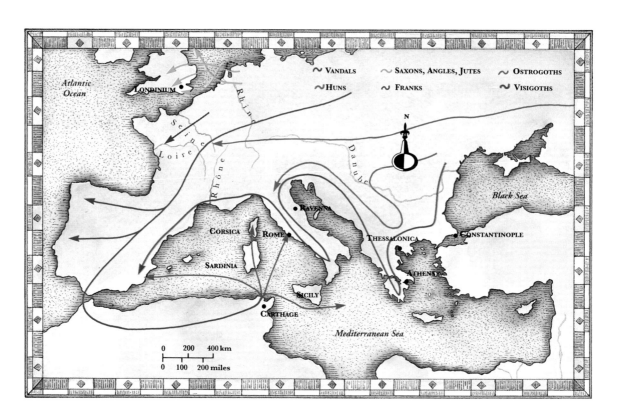

✧ THE ROMAN EMPIRE *was in turmoil during the fourth and fifth centuries, as barbarian tribes migrated westward. In about 370, the Huns arrived in southern Russia, and in the next century, led by Attila, they attacked the Eastern Roman Empire before invading Gaul. The Visigoths were admitted into the empire in 376, and under Alaric they moved west and some 30 years later sacked Rome. Later they founded a kingdom in southern France. The Vandals, another Germanic tribe, moved first to Gaul, then in the early fifth century, to northern Africa. The Ostrogoths, forced westward in the fifth century, founded a kingdom in Italy centered on Ravenna. In the same century, the Saxons, Angles, and Jutes left the continental mainland and invaded Britain.*

reunited the empire. Then in 330, he founded his new capital of Constantinople (modern Istanbul) on the site of the ancient Greek colony of Byzantium, thereby shifting the seat of imperial power eastward.

Constantine's reign was marked by a renewed confidence in Roman traditions and authority. But his death in 337 ushered in a period of uncertainty. A number of conflicts over his succession broke out, from which Constantius, his last surviving son, emerged as sole ruler. He was followed by the emperors Julian, Jovian, and Valentinian. During Valentinian's reign (364–75), the Huns, a warlike nomadic people from the Asian steppes, destroyed the kingdom of the Ostrogoths in southern Russia. This in turn resulted in the Goths, together with other Germanic tribes, migrating westward and attacking Gaul and Britain.

Under threat from these predatory tribes, Emperor Theodosius (379–95) allowed some of them to settle inside the imperial borders as *foederati*, or allies. Soon these barbarian warriors were filling the ranks of the Roman army to counter the threat of fellow German tribes: the poachers had turned gamekeepers.

Precariously reliant on barbarian manpower to safeguard its existence, the empire faced a new danger at the start of the fifth century. The Visigoths under their strong warlord Alaric invaded Italy and, in 410, captured and sacked Rome. For the next 60 years or so, the Western

Roman Empire staggered on, battered by uprisings and renewed incursions by the Vandals, Huns, and other barbarians. But in 476, the Roman army declared a German named Odoacer as their king, and he deposed the emperor, Romulus Augustulus, bringing about the end of the Western Roman Empire.

By the start of the sixth century, imperial territories in the West had been carved up into small independent Germanic kingdoms. But the ancient ways of Rome did not entirely die out. Although the material infrastructure, such as civic buildings, roads, and aqueducts, fell into neglect, the barbarians preferred to preserve other aspects of Roman civilization, rather than destroy them. They respected Roman institutions and married Roman women; and many had already been converted to the Christian faith – albeit of the heretical Arian variety – before they had crossed the imperial frontiers.

Of all the Germanic tribes that invaded western Europe, the Franks, from whom France takes its name, came to be the most important. At the end of the fifth century and at the start of the sixth, the Frankish king Clovis led his people from the Low Countries and invaded Gaul. Through his marriage to a Christian woman, Clovis was converted to the Catholic faith and was therefore supported by the Roman church in his conquests of pagan and Arian peoples.

Clovis's successors, known as the Merovingians for Merowig, Clovis's grandfather, consolidated and extended the Frankish kingdom. In time, however, they became titular monarchs only, or *rois fainéants* ("do-nothing kings"), as executive power shifted to the mayors of the royal palace. One of the most able of these mayors was Charles Martel (688–741), who in 732 defeated a Muslim army that had penetrated into southern France from Spain. His victory checked the northward advance of the Muslims into western Europe once and for all.

The Franks continued to prosper under the leadership of Charles Martel's son Pepin the Short. And in 754, Pope Stephen II bestowed a formal blessing on this latest mayor of the palace by anointing him king of the Franks. In return, Pepin agreed to fight in Italy for the papacy against its enemies the Lombards, and his victories allowed him to present the pope with lands in central Italy which became known as the papal states. The stage was now set for Pepin's son Charles, later known to the West as Charlemagne, to strengthen further the bond between the Frankish kingdom and the Catholic church.

❖ **a** MOUNTED VANDAL *leaves his villa in a sixth-century Roman mosaic (above) from Carthage, North Africa, where this fierce tribe established a kingdom. While the Vandals were ardent Arian Christians, the Frankish king Clovis I was the first barbarian sovereign to embrace Roman Catholicism. He is shown being baptized (left) in this 14th-century French illumination.*

The AGE of CHARLEMAGNE

SON OF PEPIN THE SHORT, CHARLEMAGNE, OR Charles the Great, the greatest king of the Franks, came to the throne in 768. For the next 46 years, this bull-necked warrior king applied his energy, determination, and powers of leadership to expanding the Frankish kingdom, converting the heathen, and revitalizing culture and learning, thus earning himself the sobriquet "the father of Europe."

According to the contemporary Frankish scholar Einhard, Charlemagne was a fair-haired giant of a man with a high-pitched voice and a potbelly. Physically strong, he loved hunting and swimming and was a notorious womanizer. But behind his bluff exterior he genuinely valued and aspired to intellectual and cultural pursuits. He was a native German speaker and learned Latin and some Greek, as well as being fascinated by mathematics and astrology. Although he could not write, he kept tablets under his pillow to help him learn to practice letters when the mood took him.

Like his ancestors, Charlemagne was a forceful military leader and mounted some 60 campaigns during his reign. He defeated the Avars, a nomadic people from Asia, in what is now Hungary; and he advanced into Spain to fight the Muslims, eventually making himself overlord of a small belt of land in the northeast of the country. Also, in Italy, in alliance with the papacy, he crushed the Lombards, forcing them to accept him as their king.

Perhaps his most bitter struggle was against the Saxons in northeastern Germany. For a period of about 30 years, Charlemagne fought these fierce pagans, eventually subduing them and forcibly converting them to Christianity. And he did not shrink from using extreme measures along the way: after one victory, he slaughtered 4,500 prisoners and after another deported 10,000 Saxons to the west of the Rhine.

By the year 800, Charlemagne had doubled the extent of the old Frankish kingdom. On Christmas day in the same year, while the king and his army were assembled at Mass in St. Peter's, Rome, following their successful campaign against the Lombards, Pope Leo III placed a crown on Charlemagne's head, prompting the enthusiastic Roman congregation to cry out three times: "To Charles Augustus, crowned by God, great and pacific emperor of the Romans, Life and Victory!"

Thus Charlemagne became the first emperor in the West since the deposition of Romulus Augustulus in 476 and the first emperor of the Holy Roman Empire (*opposite*). Although for the new emperor and his subjects life remained much the same, the coronation was an important moment in western history: it marked a challenge to the power and authority of the Byzantine East by the West and crystallized the notion of a Latin Christendom. It also showed how much power the papacy could – and would – wield in the creation of emperors.

Leo's motive for the coronation was not simply to bind the Christian peoples of Europe together. In 800, the Frankish kingdom was the largest and most powerful in Europe. So it also made sound political sense for the pope to look to the Frankish king for support, particularly at a time when his traditional ally in the East, the Byzantine emperor, was preoccupied with the advance of Islam. Yet Charlemagne was at pains to emphasize his independence from the papacy and interpreted the imperial title as an endorsement to rule lands other than his own.

The success of Charlemagne's reign was founded on the effectiveness of his government. His empire was divided into districts that were placed under the control of both secular and ecclesiastical authorities. And inspectors, known as *missi dominici*, were sent to each district in order to check that local officials were carrying out their duties according to the law. But perhaps his most far-sighted act was to attract renowned scholars and teachers to his court by offering them financial support.

❖ CAROLINE MINUSCULE SCRIPT, *shown in the background here, was developed during the late eighth century by Charlemagne's scholars. Its clear, compact lettering soon replaced all other writing styles in the Frankish kingdom and, by the 12th century, was favored in Ireland and England.*

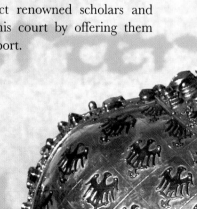

Among these men were the Italian grammarian Peter of Pisa; the historian Paul the Deacon from Lombardy; the Visigothic poet Theodulf; and, most influential of all, Alcuin of York, who advised Charlemagne on diplomatic, religious, and cultural affairs. Installed at the palace school in the imperial capital of Aachen, now in Germany, Alcuin presided over the teaching of Latin and the education of the sons of noblemen for government service.

Throughout the empire, monks were ordered to copy manuscripts of classical authors, thus preserving for posterity the works of Caesar, Tacitus, Juvenal, and others. In so doing, they developed an elegant script known as Caroline minuscule, named for Charlemagne. The development of new styles of manuscript illumination and of ecclesiastical architecture was also encouraged, laying the basis for further development later on in the Middle Ages.

The Carolingian renaissance, as the cultural revival under Charlemagne and his successors became known, lasted after the emperor's death in 814 into the reign of his son Louis the Pious. But after Louis's death in 840, the empire was divided up between his three sons. It was thus severely weakened at a time when the West faced a grave threat from the Vikings of Scandinavia, who would seriously disrupt scholarly and cultural endeavors.

❖ CHARLEMAGNE'S MAJESTY *is captured in this 14th-century reliquary bust at Aachen cathedral, Germany. As king of the Franks – the dominant European power – and Holy Roman Emperor, Charlemagne spearheaded a ninth-century renaissance of culture and political thought.*

*W*hen Charlemagne, king of the Franks, was crowned Holy Roman Emperor by Pope Leo III on Christmas day, 800 – shown below in a detail from a 15th-century French manuscript illumination – a new Christian era in Europe began. More than 300 years had elapsed since the Roman imperial title had been used in the West, and Leo III's bestowal of the crown on Charlemagne was a conscious effort on his part to revive the institution within a specifically Christian framework.

After the break-up of the Carolingian empire at the end of the ninth century, the imperial ideal was eventually revived by the German king Otto the Great, with his coronation in Rome in 962. While Otto and his immediate successors used the title of emperor as justification for German expansionism, some 200 years later Frederick I Barbarossa sought to strengthen the sacred function of the role by emphasizing its links with the ancient Roman Empire.

By the mid-14th century, with Europe's burgeoning kingdoms each attempting to assert itself, the axiom that "the king is emperor in his kingdom" held sway, effectively marking the end of an imperial, pan-European ideal. From this time until the abolition of the empire in the early 19th century, the imperial title was held largely in name only by successive dynasties of German monarchs.

❖ **a** WOODEN dRAGON **fi**GUREHEAD *was unearthed with a ninth-century Viking burial ship at Oseberg, Norway. In spite of the Northmen's reputation for relentless savagery, such intricate carvings – which may have been taken on sea journeys to deter evil spirits – have been found in surprisingly great numbers. The carved walrus ivory chess piece (right) which depicts the rook as a bearded, armed warrior, was crafted by Norwegian Vikings in the 12th century on the Isle of Lewis, Scotland.*

D URING THE NINTH CENTURY, A new prayer became common in church services all over western Europe: "*A furore Normanorum libera me, Domine*" ("From the fury of the North-men deliver me, O Lord!"). In many instances, however, the prayer was evidently unheeded as the Northmen, or Norsemen or Vikings, set out from their Scandinavian homelands to raid Britain, France, and elsewhere, "ravaging, despoiling, destroying, burning" in the words of a contemporary French monk.

The Vikings were bellicose pagan peoples from Norway, Sweden, and Denmark who, for nearly 300 years from the end of the eighth century, launched war fleets from their native fjords and harbors to attack and plunder various parts of Europe. The reasons for this sudden explosion of martial activity are still debated. If overpopulation at home was probably the main stick, the carrot was certainly the lure of booty from the monasteries and towns of western Christendom.

The start of the Vikings' reign of terror is tradition-ally dated to 793, when they descended on the monastery of Lindisfarne in northeastern England: in what became a trademark of their visits, they put monks to the sword and looted chalices, crosses, and other glittering monastic treasures.

Soon, the sight of the square, striped sails of Viking ships – high-prowed, shallow-draft vessels that could negotiate rivers – was inspiring fear in other parts of Europe. In 795, these northern warriors reached the eastern coast of Ireland – where they founded the city

tHE nORMANS

W hen the Vikings began to raid Europe's coastal settlements during the eighth and ninth centuries, those that first settled in the northwest of present-day France became known as the Normans. The duchy they founded, Normandy, formed one of the great military powers of the age.

Normandy had been first a Roman and then a Carolingian province, noted at the start of the ninth century for its monasticism. The situation changed radically when the Viking Rollo turned his attention to

the province after a long career of ravaging Ireland and the Western Isles of Scotland. He was eventually defeated at Chartres in 911 and was subsequently baptized and granted extensive lands in Normandy.

The Normans, however, were not merely warriors. The benefactions of Robert Guiscard (1015–85), conqueror of southern Italy, to the great Italian monastery of Monte Cassino made it one of the most important centers of learning and of manuscript illumination in its day. And the basilica which Guiscard had

of Dublin – and by 799 they were menacing France's Atlantic coastline.

But the Vikings were not simply thuggish agents of destruction. Many of them preferred commerce to fighting and were eager to set up trading posts and barter their furs, walrus tusks, slaves, amber, wax, and sealskins. And, from Ireland to Russia, others turned their energies to exploration and the foundation of settlements. From their base on the Shetland Islands, northeast of Scotland, they fanned out south to the Orkneys and Hebrides and northward to the Faroe Islands, reaching Iceland by about 860. Toward the end of the next century, they had colonized Greenland and by about 1000 had landed on the coast of North America.

One of the most significant Viking settlements was founded in northwestern France. In 911, the Norwegian chieftain Rollo, or Rolf, and his fellow Northmen were granted lands by the French king on either side of the Seine River and they, in return, vowed to repel any incursions by other Vikings. In time, the territory became known as Normandy – the land of the Northmen – and the Normans came to exert a major influence on western European history (*opposite*).

Between 1050 and 1100, using Normandy as their base, these fierce warriors conquered England, southern Italy, and Sicily, and fought in Wales, Scotland, and Spain. They helped to extend the power of the papacy, not least by their crucial military role in the First Crusade (pp.98–100). As a result, they established the principality of Antioch in Syria.

Swedish Vikings colonized and traded farther east. By the early 800s, they had started to move along the Dnieper River in Russia toward the Black Sea and Constantinople, where they later served as mercenaries and formed an elite guard, known as the Varangians, for the Byzantine emperor. They also used the Volga River as a highway to the Caspian Sea and the Muslim city of Baghdad, where their goods were exchanged for metals, silks, and spices from the East.

By the middle of the 11th century, Viking expansion and aggression had run out of steam. By this time, western Europe was better prepared to defend itself against attacks, and many Northmen had settled down and intermarried in the places they had formerly raided. At the same time, the Christian religion had been introduced into Scandinavia, and its teachings helped to temper the harshness of the Viking warrior life style.

constructed at Salerno in Sicily combined Norman architecture with Byzantine craftsmanship and Greek mosaics. Norman artistry is also evident in the Byzantine-style mosaics of the 12th-century cathedral of Cefalù, northern Sicily, whose twin towers (*right*) still dominate the town.

The explosion of Norman power and creativity was as short-lived as it was impressive. Yet the massive buildings the Normans have left, from England to the southern Mediterranean, are vivid reminders of one of Europe's most astonishing peoples.

PLANTAGENETS *and* CAPETIANS

O N OCTOBER 14, 1066, DUKE WILLIAM OF Normandy in northwestern France, who was of Viking descent, defeated the English king Harold at the Battle of Hastings in southern England. The battle, and the subsequent conquest of England, was a landmark in English and European history. This was because the new Norman aristocracy, with its own distinctive institutions and culture, replaced England's Anglo-Saxon and Danish ruling families and brought the country closer to mainstream continental European life.

The conquest also intertwined the fortunes of England and France more closely: from the mid-12th to the mid-15th centuries, English monarchs of the Plantagenet dynasty were also rulers of large domains in France – for which they paid homage to the French Capetian kings – and this created a constant friction between the two countries. Indeed, in the latter part of the 12th century, much of the energy of the English kings was devoted to the maintenance of their French possessions.

Anglo–French rivalry came to the fore during the reign of Henry II, the ablest of the Plantagenet kings. When he came to the English throne in 1154, Henry was already the lord of extensive lands in France. He was duke of Normandy; count of Anjou – a title inherited from his father Geoffrey Plantagenet; and his marriage to Eleanor of Aquitaine in 1152 had given him a large part of southwestern France. But although Henry ruled more land in France than the French king Louis VII himself, he nevertheless recognized Louis as his feudal overlord for those territories.

For 35 years the volatile but adroit Henry presided over his vast dominions and played an influential role on Europe's political stage. He successfully strengthened legal procedures in England and improved the country's financial affairs. One notorious blot on his reign, however, was the murder in 1170 of Thomas Becket (p.77), the archbishop of Canterbury, which sullied Henry's reputation throughout Europe. Three years later, he faced a still more serious problem when his sons – urged on by his wife Eleanor – and their allies initiated rebellions against him. Henry, however, rallied his forces and managed to defeat the rebels one at a time. Afterward, while showing considerable leniency toward his sons, he ordered Eleanor to be placed in confinement.

In spite of Henry's political troubles, Louis VII was in too weak a position to gain any advantage from them. But

❖ **tHE tomb figures** *of King Henry II of England (1154–89) and his wife, Eleanor of Aquitaine, lie peacefully in the church at Fontevrault, western France. Their tranquil expressions form a striking contrast to the couple's turbulent lives: their marital strife was legendary, and Eleanor even urged each of their four sons into rebellion against their father.*

after Louis's death in 1180, his successor Philip II Augustus proved to be more able: in 1188 he allied himself with Henry's eldest surviving son, Richard the Lion-Hearted (pp.98–100), and together they fought and defeated the aging Henry, who was left with no choice but to accept Richard as his sole heir. A year later, exhausted and embittered, Henry died.

The first truly effective king of the Capetian dynasty, Philip Augustus went on to reconquer many of the French territories held by the English. From 1202 to 1204, he invaded and captured Normandy and took control of Maine, Anjou, and Touraine. Then in 1214, at the Battle of Bouvines, he decisively defeated a combined force brought together by the English king John, who had succeeded his brother Richard in 1199 and was determined to retake his French domains. The following year, Philip's son Louis invaded England and, on the death of John in 1216, was close to taking the English crown for the Capetians. However, the minority government of Henry III and the papacy united against him, and he withdrew in 1217.

Philip died in 1223, nine years after Bouvines. His successor, Louis VIII, ruled for three years before Louis IX, the best-loved Capetian king, came to the throne. Louis was a pious Christian – he was acclaimed as a saint after his death – and a fair administrator of justice. He also won himself a reputation as a charismatic commander: in 1229, at the age of 15, he headed a French army that compelled an invasion force under Henry III of England to retreat across the English Channel. And in 1242, he again decisively defeated Henry on French soil and forced him to retire to England.

Louis was zealous in his fight against the Muslims – he led the unsuccessful Seventh Crusade against them in 1248 – and equally determined to live at peace with his Christian neighbors. He tried, for example, to forge a lasting peace with Henry III. By the Treaty of Paris in 1259, Louis agreed to let Henry retain Gascony on condition that he acknowledge his status as a vassal of the French crown.

These were generous terms, since Louis could probably have taken Henry's French possessions by force. However, the continuing English foothold in France would prove a source of future tension – tension that would erupt during the 14th and 15th centuries in the great Anglo–French struggle which later became known as the Hundred Years' War (pp.110–11).

❖ KING PHILIP II, *shown (left below) at his coronation in 1179 at Rheims in this 15th-century illumination, made huge gains against England in the fight for control of French lands. Another strong Capetian monarch was Louis IX, whose palace chapel, the Sainte-Chapelle in Paris, was famed for its stained glass (below) and large collection of holy relics.*

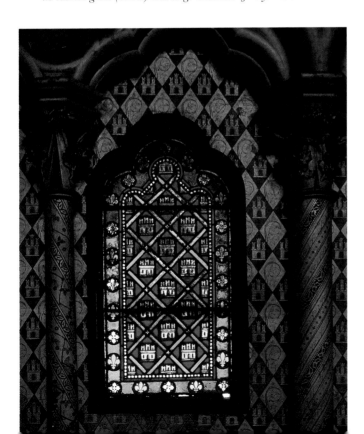

CITY STATES *of* ITALY

*T*HROUGHOUT THE MIDDLE AGES, THE ITALIAN peninsula was a stage for intense political and social drama characterized by incessant inter-city fighting, complex political alliances, and yet – for much of the time – economic prosperity. In the north, Venice and Genoa rose to prominence on the back of extensive maritime trade in the Mediterranean, and other cities, such as Milan in Lombardy, became important in the growing resistance against the territorial claims of the Holy Roman Emperors (pp.10–11).

In the center of the country, Rome was still wrapped in the mystique of its former classical glory, and for most of the medieval period was the seat of the popes, who held sway over the Christian faithful throughout Latin Christendom. Meanwhile, in the south of Italy, the dominant power was the kingdom of Naples which, at various times during the course of its history, was united with the island of Sicily.

The patterns of medieval Italian society began to coalesce during the 11th century when, in the north, there was a marked increase in the number of communes – towns that had obtained the right to govern themselves. This was partly due to the lack of a strong central authority, but also because the citizens felt the need to protect themselves from the local nobles.

In the same century, Venice, situated on the Po estuary in the northeast of the country, became prosperous from trade in the eastern Mediterranean, especially after 1081, when it won lucrative trading concessions with the Byzantine capital of Constantinople. And Venice's wealth continued to grow during the Crusades (pp.98–100), when it established commercial enclaves in Tyre and Acre on the Palestinian coast.

In the 12th and 13th centuries, the cities of northern Italy faced a political crisis when they were threatened by the expansionist ambitions of the Holy Roman

❖ ꜰREDERICK ɪ ʙARBAROSSA,
German king and Holy Roman Emperor from 1152, sits between his sons in this 12th-century depiction.

Emperors. In particular, Emperor Frederick I Barbarossa (1152–90), eager to restore the powers and lands of the empire, mounted a number of expeditions to assert his authority in Lombardy. In 1158, he successfully besieged Milan and, later, gained control of other cities, where he proceeded to install his own magistrates, or *podestàs*.

In 1167, however, 16 northern cities, backed by Frederick's enemy, Pope Alexander III, formed an alliance known as the Lombard League to recover their freedom. A showdown with Frederick was inevitable. It came on May 29, 1176: at the Battle of Legnano, Frederick fought the forces of the league and was decisively beaten. After this, he was compelled to make humiliating overtures of peace to Alexander and actually prostrated himself before the pope's feet outside the entrance of St. Mark's church in Venice.

However, imperial interference in Italian affairs continued with the accession of Barbarossa's grandson, Frederick II, in 1212. The new emperor's struggle with the papacy enlarged the split of Italian nobles and cities into two separate warring factions: the Guelphs (pro-papal) and the Ghibellines (pro-imperial). Even after Frederick's death in 1250, the fighting between these two factions continued, despite their severance from their original political origins.

In the next century, wars between city states – often conducted by hired mercenaries under commanders known as *condottieri* – were rife, increasing the political turmoil. Then, in 1348, the Black Death struck, devastating the country, in some areas killing as much as half the population.

By the early 1400s, five major centers of power had emerged in the peninsula: Florence, which came under the control of the Medici family in 1434; Venice, a republic headed by the doge, who was elected for life; Milan, under the sway of the Visconti family; Naples, which was taken over by the Aragonese of Spain under

Alfonso the Magnanimous in 1442; and Rome, the seat of the papacy, which was increasingly becoming the prey of political factions.

Despite the ravages of the plague and continued internal warfare – in 1423, Florence and Milan fought each other in a war that eventually involved Venice and, later, Naples – cities remained wealthy. Increased trade with the Middle East was partly the reason for this, but the prosperity of great banking centers in Florence, Genoa, Lucca, and elsewhere was also a contributory factor.

This prosperity helped to nurture the Renaissance. This was the rebirth of classical learning and a flowering of art and culture which, from its early beginnings in the 14th century, had gathered momentum to become firmly established in Italy during the course of the 15th century.

✧ **bYZANTINE mOSAICS** *depict the main incidents of the Bible on the ceiling of St. Mark's Basilica in Venice. The present basilica dates from the 11th century, and the mosaics were added over several centuries, a testament to Venice's trading and cultural links with Constantinople.*

fIRST lIGHT OF THE rENAISSANCE

*t*he renowned Italian artist Giotto di Bondone (1267–1337), depicted above by the 15th-century Italian painter Paolo Uccello, was born the son of a field worker in the town of Vespignano, 14 miles (23 km) from Florence. He stands at the threshold of the medieval and modern worlds of painting, rejecting the formal style typical of medieval art in favor of a hitherto unknown dramatic and emotional realism.

Giotto's fame spread in his own lifetime. He was mentioned by Dante in his *Divine Comedy,* and in 1550, the Italian artist and biographer Giorgio Vasari began his famous history of Italian art with Giotto, citing him as the man who broke away from the Middle Ages and ushered in the "good modern manner."

It is said that at the age of 10, Giotto was discovered by

the noted Florentine artist Cimabue sketching a lamb in a field. The older artist was himself experimenting with more naturalistic forms of art, and he trained the boy, who went on to realize his master's aspirations.

Giotto painted frescoes – murals on wet plaster – in chapels in Assisi, Rome, Padua, Florence, and Naples. These delicate, colorful paintings show Giotto's revolutionary approach to art: stylized background and clothing detail is kept to a minimum while the expressions and gestures show the characters' feelings.

Nor was Giotto simply a painter: in 1334, he was put in charge of the building of Florence's cathedral, or duomo. He designed several sculptures for the outside of the building as well as the campanile (bell tower), which is still known today as "Giotto's Tower."

GIOTTO

The role of the CHURCH

THE POWER STRUGGLE BETWEEN POPES AND SECULAR rulers – especially the Holy Roman Emperors (pp.10–11) – was one of the most enduring and far-reaching issues during the course of the Middle Ages. When Pope Leo III gave the full weight of papal endorsement to Charlemagne, king of the Franks, by crowning him emperor in Rome in 800 in return for his military protection, he was also sowing the seeds of future conflict between the papacy and empire: who was supreme over whom?

In the 10th and early 11th centuries, the weakness of the papacy and the need for reform within the church safe-guarded imperial prerogatives. Popes had by and large become puppets whose strings were controlled by powerful Roman nobles. The house of Tusculum, for example, nearly turned the papacy into a family business by pro-ducing three popes in a row.

At the same time, the reputation of the church was suffering from other abuses, especially simony – the sale or purchase of church offices – and clerical marriage. The objection to priests marrying was based on both spiri-tual considerations – that chastity was a more holy and fitting condition for a priest in his conduct of otherworldly duties – and practical ones: an unmarried priest could devote more time to his flock and would not be tempted to use the material benefits of his office to provide for his wife and children. But an ineffective papacy made little headway against these problems.

In 1049, however, the election of the strong, energetic Pope Leo IX set the papacy on the road to reform. Not content with staying in Rome like his predecessors, Leo decided to tour other parts of Europe to assert his moral and spiritual authority in person. On October 1, 1049, he reached the town of Rheims in France, where he com-bined the consecration of a new church with the meeting of an ecclesiastical council.

Those who attended the council were in for a shock: Leo demanded that all the abbots and bishops present should publicly swear that they had not bought their offices. One bishop immediately fled the church and another, who stood up to defend his colleague, was struck dumb. Even the archbishop of Rheims asked for a day to consider his reply. As cleric after cleric came forward to confess, it was clear that here was a pope who was made of sterner moral stuff than his predecessors.

✧ POPE GREGORY VII, *seated with a scribe in this 11th-century illumination, made enemies of emperors and kings by his reforming zeal.*

✧ THE MASSIVE ROUND WALLS *of Castel Sant'Angelo – the fortified papal palace near the Vatican – overlook the Tiber River. The structure was first a Roman mausoleum, then a fortress, before becoming a papal palace, with sumptuous apartments and a dungeon, in the 13th century.*

Leo's reforms increased the prestige and self-confidence of the papacy, a process continued under the pontificate of Hildebrand, who was elected Pope Gregory VII in 1073, and under whom the clash between popes and emperors came to a head. Gregory spoke out in the strongest terms against clerical marriages and simony and re-emphasized the importance of canon law. This was the mass of rules and regulations derived from the Bible, the early church fathers, papal letters, and other sources, concerning practical church matters such as the discipline of errant clergy and the collection and distribution of tithes and alms.

Gregory's drive to reform and purify the church of secular influence led to what later became known as the "investiture contest." Because bishops and abbots were often at the same time powerful landlords commanding great estates and human resources, it was naturally in the interest of kings and emperors to appoint clergy who were sympathetic to their cause – their power to appoint being realized when they "invested" them with the insignia of their offices.

But Gregory was resolutely opposed to the practice of lay investiture and in 1075 issued a papal decree forbidding it. This ruling dealt a heavy blow to the Holy Roman Emperor Henry IV, who needed the support of his bishops at home in Germany, where powerful nobles posed a potential threat to his rule. In 1076, backed by his German bishops, Henry declared Gregory a "false monk" and urged him to relinquish his position as pope. Gregory, however, responded quickly by excommunicating Henry and forbidding anyone to serve him as king – an act that spurred Henry's enemies in Germany to revolt, forcing the king to climb down and seek an audience with Gregory to beg his forgiveness.

On January 25, 1077, Henry arrived at the castle of Canossa in the Apennines, where Gregory was staying at the time. For three days, the pope let the humiliated emperor stand outside the castle walls, barefoot in the snow, before finally admitting him and releasing him from his excommunication.

But the conflict did not stop there. Three years later, once more angered by the contemptuous attitude Henry showed toward the papacy, Gregory again excommunicated him. This time, however, Henry decided to invade Rome and successfully deposed his old enemy, forcing him into exile.

But the argument over lay investiture continued to rumble on after Gregory's death in 1085. Eventually a compromise was reached in the Concordat of Worms in 1122. It was agreed that the church, not the emperor, should elect bishops and abbots and invest them with the ring and staff, symbols of their spiritual authority, while the emperor could invest them with the scepter, the symbol of secular authority.

The concordat went some way to defusing the pope–emperor conflict but did not put an end to it. Elsewhere, in France and England, relations between kings and popes remained highly sensitive, despite the fact that agreements similar to the Concordat of Worms had been reached with both countries in 1106–7.

After Worms, however, the papacy's star was in the ascendant for the rest of the century, rising to its highest point with the accession of Innocent III in 1198. A Roman of noble blood, Innocent influenced the election of emperors; presided over the Fourth Crusade; led the drive against heretics; gave support to saints Francis and Dominic and their followers; and, in 1215, convened the Fourth Lateran Council at which important decrees concerning reforms and doctrines were issued. The medieval papacy had now reached the zenith of its spiritual and temporal power.

❖ POPE INNOCENT III (1161–1216) – *shown here in a fresco detail from the church of Sacro Speco, Subiaco, Italy – raised the medieval papacy to its most prestigious level. His administrative talents and insistence on church law reasserted papal supremacy over secular monarchs and the Holy Roman Emperor.*

*I*N THE NINTH CENTURY, AT A TIME WHEN *VIKINGS* from Scandinavia were raiding and plundering western Europe, a group from Sweden – known as Varangians – set out eastward into what is now Russia. They fought and defeated communities of Slav peoples living near the rivers they used as highways into the interior, and founded trading posts.

In about 862, Rurik, leader of the Varangian Rus tribe – from whom later Russian nobles were keen to trace their descent – occupied what is now Novgorod, near the Baltic Sea. Then 20 years later, other Rus Varangians captured Kiev on the Dnieper River and made it the capital of the first Russian state, also known as Kiev.

Well situated for the Baltic–Black Sea and east–west trade, the city of Kiev grew in wealth and prestige, and its princes were able to extend their control eastward and northward over other Rus principalities. During the 10th century, it began to forge trading and political links with Byzantium, and in 988 the Grand Prince Vladimir was converted by Byzantine missionaries to the Orthodox church. Vladimir also married the sister of Basil II, the Byzantine emperor, and introduced Byzantine church ritual and architecture into Russian religious life.

Kiev reached the peak of its power during the first half of the 11th century under its greatest ruler, Yaroslav the Wise. At this time, the first Russian law code was drawn up, and educational establishments were founded. The city itself was a major center for trade in sable, fox, and other furs and reputedly had as many as 400 churches and 8 large markets. Its population may have been as high as 20,000 people, making it comparable in size to the largest cities in western Europe.

In the 12th century, however, Kiev began to decline through a combination of internal fighting among its rulers, a reduction in trade – partly due to the competition from Venice and Genoa in the west – and ferocious raids by Mongols and other nomadic Asiatic peoples. There were also a number of attacks from the west, with various incursions by Swedes, Lithuanians, and the German Teutonic Knights (*opposite*).

As the centralized power of Kiev diminished, its lands began to splinter into separate principalities. In the north,

❖ **lORD nOVGOROD tHE gREAT**, *as this Russian town was known in the Middle Ages, was the largest settlement in northern Russia by the 12th century. Originally a ninth-century Viking trading post, Novgorod became a self-governing region in the 11th century, and through its trade with the Hanseatic League, the town became immensely wealthy. Some of that wealth was used to build churches, such as the one here, whose distinctive onion domes still grace the city's skyline.*

Novgorod declared its independence in 1136 and later profited from its association with the German town of Lübeck, one of the leading members of the Hanseatic League (pp.58–59). South of Novgorod, the town of Vladimir rose to prominence when Prince Andrey Bogolyubsky made it his capital in the principality of Vladimir–Suzdal, having sacked Kiev in 1169.

Then, in the 13th century, Kiev's fortunes went from bad to worse. In 1236, the Mongols – also known as the Tatars – invaded Kiev, sacked its towns and, in 1240, destroyed the city itself. They then went on to establish in southern and eastern Russia their empire of the Golden Horde, which lasted until 1480.

However, the Mongol period was not totally disastrous for Russia. Local princes were allowed to continue ruling, and the Mongols proved remarkably tolerant of the Russian church. And it was during this time that Moscow began to rise to prominence. Situated near productive farm lands and having access to major rivers, the city was well placed to benefit from trade, especially with the Crimea region and with Constantinople.

In the 1300s, the grand dukes of Moscow, although paying tribute to their Tatar overlords, increased their influence, and under Ivan I (1328–41), the city established control over the whole province of Moscow. Then in 1380, Dmitri Donskoy struck a blow against Mongol domination when he defeated the Tatars at Kulikovo on the Don River. As Mongol power began to wane and Lithuania adopted Roman Catholicism (1386–87), Moscow became the spiritual center of the Russian Orthodox church.

In 1408, the city fought off another Mongol attack, and during the rest of the century, it grew in size and power as palaces, churches, and monasteries were constructed. In 1478, Ivan III the Great (1462–1505) annexed Novgorod and, in 1485, Tver, giving reality to his title of Grand Duke of all Russia; and in 1480 he refused to pay tribute to the Mongols. These developments paved the way for the reign of Ivan IV the Terrible (1533–84), the first tsar of Russia.

GERMAN CRUSADERS

*t*he spirit of the Christian Crusades in the Holy Land (pp.98–100) was carried into the deep forests of northeastern Europe by a dedicated band of warriors known as the Order of Teutonic Knights. Between the 12th and the 16th centuries, these heavily armored soldiers, shown in this 15th-century German illumination (*right*) wearing their distinctive white cloaks with black crosses, carved out a huge Christian dominion comprising most of the Baltic coast, Prussia, Lithuania, and parts of Russia.

Founded as a charitable order in the Holy Land in 1190, the Teutonic Knights assumed military status soon after. In 1211, they moved to eastern Europe in search of new challenges after the failure of the Crusades. With an army of German recruits, they fought as mercenaries for the Christian cause against the pagan tribes in modern Poland and blazed a trail for German expansion on the eastern frontier.

Within 50 years, they had established control over Prussia in northern Germany and formed an alliance with an earlier German order of knights called the Brothers of the Sword, who controlled the eastern Baltic lands. In 1242, in an attempt to seize the Russian city of Novgorod, they fought an army under Alexander Nevsky, who defeated the knights on the frozen ice of Lake Peipus: their military ambitions in Russia had been broken forever.

During the 14th century, the order concentrated its efforts on conquering Lithuania, then the last remaining pagan nation in Europe. Although Lithuania was converted to Christianity in 1386–7, continuing skirmishes led to a resounding defeat for the Teutonic Knights by the combined forces of Lithuania and Poland at Tannenberg in 1410. They lost their grand master and hundreds of their crack troops. From this point onward, the Teutonic Knights declined in power and influence, and the order was eventually formally dissolved in 1561.

The ɪBERIAN CʀUCIBLE

*T*HE DOMINANT THEME IN SPAIN DURING THE Middle Ages was the *Reconquista* – the reconquest by Spanish Christian armies of territories held by the Moors, Muslims who had invaded the Iberian peninsula from northern Africa in the early eighth century. Before the arrival of the Moors, Spain was under the control of the Visigoths, a Germanic people who had crossed the Pyrenees in 456 and settled with the native Spanish–Roman inhabitants.

In 711, however, a power struggle within the Visigothic kingdom ended with one faction seeking military aid from Muslims in Morocco. These Arabs and Berbers duly crossed the Strait of Gibraltar, but then proceeded to exceed their brief: they wrested power from the Visigoths and, by 718, had conquered most of the peninsula.

Moorish power and influence then developed further from 756, when Abd ar-Rahman I arrived in Spain from Damascus, Syria, where his Umayyad dynasty had been deposed as caliphs, or spiritual leaders, of the Muslim world. Abd ar-Rahman made his capital at Córdoba in Andalusia, southern Spain, and this city became the most sophisticated in western Europe.

During the next three centuries, the foundations of Spain's complex medieval culture, in which Muslims, Mozarabs – Christians under Muslim rule – and Jews all made their contributions, were laid. For example, in Toledo, recaptured by the Christians during the late 11th century, Islamic texts on science and mathematics, some of them preserving Greek knowledge, were translated from the Arabic.

The Moors themselves produced great thinkers, none more so than Averroës (1126–98), who lived in Seville and Córdoba and whose commentaries on Aristotle provided western Europe with its first main introduction to this great Greek philosopher. The Jews, with their knowledge of Hebrew, Arabic, and Latin, also made an important contribution. In particular, Moses Maimonides (1135–1204) formulated a structure of religious thought that sustained contemporary Jews.

Córdoba began to decline in the early 11th century, and this resulted in the rise of local Muslim kings, or *taifas*, who fought among themselves, often hiring Christian troops to help them. With the fragmentation of Muslim power, the Christian king Alfonso VI of León and Castile exploited the Moors' rivalries and captured Toledo in 1085. The victory, however, spurred the Moors into appealing to a Moroccan dynasty known as the Almoravids for help. These aggressive Muslims of Berber stock crossed over to the peninsula and proceeded to keep the Christians at bay, as did the Almohads, the dynasty that succeeded them.

However, the *Reconquista* again gathered pace in the early 13th century, when the Christians decisively defeated an Almohad army at the Battle of Las Navas de Tolosa in 1212, a victory that opened the way for the reconquest of Andalusia. Ferdinand III, who reunited the realms of León and Castile, took Córdoba in 1236, Jaén in 1246, and, two years later, Seville. The shrinking Moorish kingdom was now centered on Granada.

But it was only a matter of time before the city, with its celebrated fortress-palace, the

❖ **ʟ**ᴇᴀᴅɪɴɢ **ғ**ɪɢᴜʀᴇs *in the final reconquest of Spain from the Moors, King Ferdinand II and Queen Isabella, shown in this 15th-century illumination, were genuinely devoted to each other despite the fact that their marriage had been arranged. After Isabella died in 1504, Ferdinand requested in his will that he be buried next to his wife at Granada, where they had forced the Moors' final surrender in 1492.*

❖ **ᴏ**ʀɴᴀᴛᴇ **ᴍ**ᴏᴏʀɪsʜ **ᴀ**ʀᴄʜᴇs *supported by elegant marble columns enclose the Court of Lions in the Alhambra, Granada. This Moorish fortified palace was begun in the mid-13th century and fell to the Christians in 1492. In spite of later Christian alterations, the Alhambra, with its pools, splashing fountains, and lacelike carvings, remains a stunning example of Moorish architecture.*

Alhambra, would fall to the Christians. The marriage of Ferdinand II of Aragon and Isabella of Castile in 1469 marked a critical point. Backed by powerful resources and driven by a vision of a unified Christian Spain, the Catholic Monarchs, as they were known, prepared to take the sole remaining outpost of Islam. In January 1492, the moment came: Boabdil, the last Muslim ruler in Spain, surrendered Granada.

As a silver cross and the banner of Saint James were raised on one of the Alhambra's towers, a new page in Spain's history was turned. And the same year marked the beginning of a new chapter in world history: for Isabella agreed to support the Genoese sailor Christopher Columbus in his exploratory voyage westward across the Atlantic. Columbus's "discovery" of the New World and the subsequent opening up of its interior and the formation of empires led Europeans from the introspection of the Middle Ages into a new era characterized by energy and expansion.

EL CID

*t*he brilliant 11th-century soldier Rodrigo Diaz, popularly known as El Cid, became a national hero in the reconquest of Spain. His burial place at the monastery of San Pedro de Cardena, near Burgos in Castile, a detail of which is shown above, was a popular pilgrimage destination.

Rodrigo was born into a minor noble family in about 1043. He was highly ambitious and early on gained favor from the Castilian king, Sancho II, for whom he led a successful campaign against Alfonso VI of León. But he was placed in a precarious position after Sancho's assassination and Alfonso's return to power as king of both León and Castile. Despite an attempted reconciliation with Alfonso, distrust between the two men forced Rodrigo into the Muslim kingdom of Saragossa, northeastern Spain, in 1081.

Rodrigo then spent a decade fighting for the Muslims, during which he acquired the Arabic name *al-sayyid,* "lord," which was hispanicized to El Cid. So impressive was his reputation that in 1086, when Alfonso was faced with an invasion by the Almoravids of northern Africa, Rodrigo was recalled from exile.

Two years later, although still fighting under Alfonso's banner, El Cid was planning to take Valencia from the Moors for himself. After an epic siege in 1093, he entered the city in triumph. From then until his death in 1099, El Cid held the city nominally for Alfonso, but in practice as ruler.

⚜ **COURTLY FIGURES** *converse in view of the Chateau of Dourdan, France, in this page from the Duc de Berry's* Très Riches Heures *(15th century).*

CASTLES, NOBLES, AND KNIGHTS

" All the way… I never once let

my eyes turn back towards Joinville,

for fear my heart might be filled with longing

at the thought of my lovely castle ."

From the *Life of Saint Louis* by Jean de Joinville (*c.*1224–1319)

NOTHING EPITOMIZES THE MIDDLE Ages more concretely than the castle. From Ireland to Palestine, the remains of great stone towers, crenellated walls, gateways, and moats are still resonant of a society in which local power was very much commensurate with sheer physical strength.

Often strategically sited on hilltops, strongholds such as Chateau Gaillard in France and Dover Castle in England gave military muscle and control to the kings and lords who built them. But they also served as the residences of royalty and noblemen, who formed an elite stratum in a society in which the armored cavalryman, or knight, was the most powerful martial figure. Knights were trained in the arts of fighting from a young age, and their preparation for war included taking part in tournaments – events that were as much festive occasions as displays of jousting and other martial skills.

Medieval society was meshed together by a web of personal relationships between kings, princes, noblemen, and the clergy. The essence of the relationship consisted of a king or lord granting a unit of land, or fief, to another nobleman or freeman in return for military or other services. Later historians described this system of reciprocity as "feudal" – a word derived from *feudum*, the Latin word for a fief. In reality, however, feudal society was never a neatly worked-out system. And eventually, it was fatally undermined by the rise of strong centralized monarchies and the growth of the town, which replaced the lord's castle as the focal point for medieval life.

KEEPS and STRONGHOLDS

*I*N THE 14TH-CENTURY ENGLISH ARTHURIAN ROMANCE *Sir Gawain and the Green Knight*, the eponymous hero seeking the domain of the mysterious Green Knight comes across a magnificent castle. From the waters of the moat a huge stone wall rises up, punctuated by turrets. Inside the walls, the main hall looms up, encrusted with towers and turrets and edged with crenellations. So many brightly painted pinnacles were clustered together that the castle looked as if it had been "cut out of paper."

Castles are one of the most evocative images of the Middle Ages. Whether they are the highly ornamented late medieval fortresses in the manner of Gawain's castle or the simple fortified towers found in Scotland and Italy, their dank, broken-down carcasses litter the fields and hilltops of Europe. Others rise like operatic sets with the restorations and embellishments of later centuries that evoke both the power and the often rudimentary living conditions of medieval kings, princes, and lords.

The earliest castles of the Middle Ages – known as motte and bailey – bore little resemblance to their grandiose descendants. They were relatively simple in design and were also quick and economical to erect – factors that made them attractive to Duke William of Normandy, who put up large numbers of them after his conquest of England in 1066. A circular or oval ditch was dug, with the earth heaped up in the center to form a motte, or mound. On top of this, a wooden tower that was enclosed by a palisade was constructed. The motte was then connected

⚜ **NORMAN WORKERS** *shovel earth to build a motte and bailey castle at Hastings, England, in 1066, shown in the Bayeux Tapestry. Such castles provided bases for the Normans as they invaded the country.*

to an outer enclosure, or bailey, which was also protected by a ditch and palisade. This provided an area where animals could be kept or where peasants could shelter in the event of an attack.

From the late 11th century to the end of the Middle Ages, castles became more elaborate in their attempts to adapt to improved siege techniques; and they also varied in style from country to country and according to the terrain.

The motte and bailey plan evolved into the stone shell keep, as at Gisors, France; a much more robust version was the rectangular keep, or *donjon*, as found at Rochester, England. Later these became round or polygonal in shape, deflecting missiles and resisting mining operations more effectively. Sturdy stone "curtain" walls were raised around the baileys, and this extra degree of protection allowed the buildings within to become less martial and more suited to the comforts of everyday living.

One of the finest examples of state-of-the-art castle technology is Chateau Gaillard in Normandy, France, built between 1196 and 1198 by Richard I, the Lion-Hearted, king of England, who ruled this part of the country as its duke. Richard took such a personal interest in the work that a contemporary chronicler wrote that if an angel had told him to abandon it, "that angel would have been met by a volley of curses."

The castle stands dramatically on a precipitous cliff 300 feet (90 m) above the Seine River. Three distinct enclosures – the outer, middle, and inner baileys – were

⚜ **CASTEL dELL'OVA** *in Naples, Italy, looms from a rocky outcrop that was once an island, but is now joined to the mainland. Begun in 1154 by William I, the Norman king of Sicily, Castel dell'Ova has the austere square towers typical of later Norman castle building.*

protected both by moats and by curtain walls fortified by circular towers. The keep, which is constructed at the edge of the precipice, had so-called battered walls. These sloped steeply outward toward the bottom to deter the enemy from using scaling ladders and from mounting mining operations. And machicolations – stone structures projecting from the top of the walls – allowed defenders to rain boiling oil and missiles on besiegers.

Both the size and prestige of castles depended very much on the status, energy, and wealth of the kings and noblemen who commissioned them. Two of the greatest castle builders of the period were the Holy Roman Emperor Frederick II (1220–50) and the English king Edward I (1272–1307). Frederick, whose territories encompassed Sicily as well as various parts of Italy, built an array of fine fortresses, including Castel del Monte in Apulia and Catania in Sicily. All his castles were symmetrical and well proportioned and they showed knowledge of the structure of Muslim and Byzantine fortresses of the Middle East, perhaps as a result of Frederick's experiences on Crusade in the Holy Land (pp.98–100).

Crusader castles, in particular those built by the Knights Templar and Hospitaler, exerted a great influence on western architects. At Krak des Chevaliers in Syria and at other castles, the keep became a bastion of linked towers and was enclosed by concentric curtain walls encrusted with towers.

Edward I, who was also a Crusader, is most famous for the castles he built in Wales. Indeed, some scholars believe them to be the greatest of the Middle Ages. Designed to subdue the rebellious Welsh, these fortresses, especially Caernarfon – where an enemy had to negotiate a combination of five doors, two drawbridges, and six portcullises – Beaumaris, and Conway, are vivid reminders of Edward's military resolve.

Perhaps the most impressive of Edward's castles was Harlech. Begun in 1283 and situated on a crag that overlooks Cardigan Bay, it cost the then enormous sum of about £8,000. Its curtain walls were 12 feet (3.5 m) or more thick, and it was protected at its four corners by round turreted towers. On the eastern face of the castle, the entrance was fortified by a tall twin-towered gatehouse, which gave it the features of a keep – a development that also occurred in other English castles. The idea was that by thrusting the headquarters of the castle into the curtain wall, the commander would be able to take a more active role in the direction of counter-siege operations.

During 1294, Harlech's defenses were put to the test: the Welsh prince Madoc attacked it with his army. He was held off, however, by a defending force of only 37 men.

In addition to being bastions of defense, castles were also used as forward and support bases in offensive operations, and in peace time, as centers of local administration. They were the residences of the aristocratic elite and also served as treasuries, prisons, and munitions stores.

Castle interiors had wooden floors and small unglazed windows that were eventually filled with semi-opaque glass. Walls were plastered and painted and sometimes covered with tapestries or embroidered hangings; fires provided heat and light. The main room was the Great Hall, situated in the keep. Here the lord of the castle conducted his affairs, ate, and entertained.

BUILT BY the English king Richard I in the late 12th century, Chateau Gaillard in northwestern France was besieged successfully only once – by the French in 1203, who demolished large parts of the walls by relentless assault with mines and catapults.

☙ tHE 15TH-CENTURY *castle
at Coca in Spain took military
architecture to new heights of
elaboration. While its ornate
brickwork incorporates*

*Moorish decorative styles more
befitting a palace than a castle,
the massive, sloping lower wall
was intended to withstand sieges
as well as to impress.*

A typical daily routine for a nobleman would start at dawn with Mass in the chapel. He would then take a light breakfast before attending to the affairs of the day, such as the administration of his estates. A large meal was served at about midday, after which he might go off to hunt – usually deer – or perhaps hawk, ride, or fence. Supper was served after sunset, accompanied by singing in the Great Hall's gallery. After dinner entertainment on some days might include jugglers, acrobats, singers, and harpists.

The heyday of the castle extended from the 12th to the 14th centuries. During the 15th century, however, the rise of towns, together with the dwindling of hierarchical feudal ties (pp.36–37) and increasingly advanced firearms, contributed to the castle's gradual fall from supremacy. Its two functions – both as a residence and as a fortress – were replaced, respectively, by the manor house and by military fortifications, which were designed increasingly to be defended by artillery.

D over Castle is shown overlooking the English Channel to the south in the photograph (*previous page*). When the castle was converted to an artillery fortress in the late 18th century, its towers and crenellated walls were lowered, and the keep was strengthened to support a gun platform.

In this reconstruction, the castle is shown at its military height in the mid-13th century. King Henry III, with his barons in attendance, is shown. Their retinues are accommodated in tents situated in a section of the outer bailey, or enclosure (*far right*), while armorers and grooms occupy an area beside St. Mary's church (*center background*).

The huge rectangular keep (*center*) is protected by two "curtain" walls, which are punctuated by overhanging towers. The northern entrance to the inner bailey is protected by a courtyard, or barbican, which one of the barons and his retinue are entering (*center*). The cluster of towers known as the Norfolk Towers (*left foreground*) formed the castle's original entrance. But after the siege of 1216, the Constable's Gate (*far right*), with its five towers projecting over the moat, was built as the new entrance.

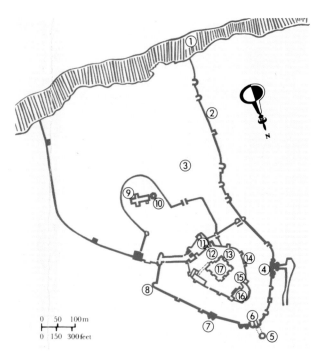

✣ dOVER CASTLE'S *most important defenses in the medieval period are indicated on the ground plan:* **1** *Cliff face* **2** *Outer curtain wall* **3** *Outer bailey* **4** *Constable's Gate* **5** *St. John's Tower* **6** *Norfolk Towers* **7** *Fitzwilliam Gate* **8** *Avranches Tower* **9** *St. Mary's Church* **10** *Roman pharos* **11** *Southern barbican* **12** *Palace Gate* **13** *Inner bailey* **14** *Inner curtain wall* **15** *King's Gate* **16** *Northern barbican* **17** *Keep*

Dubbed the "key of England" by a 13th-century English chronicler, Dover Castle is one of the most powerful and extensive fortresses in Europe. Its hilltop site, on the coast of Kent, commands a harbor and the shortest sea crossing to France, and its strategic importance was recognized long before the Middle Ages.

From prehistoric times to the fifth century A.D., Celts, Romans, and Saxons all contributed to the site's defenses. But the story of the impressive structures still crowning the cliffs above Dover begins after the victory of William of Normandy over the English army at Hastings in 1066. William then set about rebuilding the existing Saxon fort as a classic motte and bailey (mound and courtyard) structure, and this provided him with a secure base from which he could mount his march inland to subdue the rest of the country.

But it was William's great-grandson, Henry II (1154–89), who made the castle arguably the strongest in England. With stone ferried across the English Channel from Caen in Normandy, Henry built a huge square tower, or keep, which rises more than 80 feet (24 m) above its sloping plinth. Its walls, varying in thickness between 17 and 21 feet (5 and 6.5 m), provided a formidable last line of defense, as well as storage and accommodation for the garrison. Surrounding the keep were two rings of walls punctuated by projecting towers that gave the defenders a clear field of fire against besiegers.

Henry spent a total of £6,000 on Dover – an expenditure that far exceeded that on any other castle in England. In comparison, Maurice, Henry's architect/mason, was paid the princely sum of one shilling per day, about £18 for a year's work.

The castle faced its first serious threat during the reign of Henry's son, John (1199–1216). In 1216, Prince Louis of France, encouraged by certain English barons, arrived in England to seize John's crown. Although the French reduced part of Dover's gateway to rubble, the defenders managed to fill the breach with a wooden barricade and saved the day. Prince Louis continued the siege until the death of John brought to the throne the young Henry III, who had the support of a number of powerful barons.

Alarmed by the castle's apparent vulnerability, the new king's council spent another £7,500 refortifying it. The old gateway was blocked up, and a new one, the elaborate Constable's Gate, was built on the western side – it still remains the main entrance. By the mid-1250s, the castle had reached its greatest size and strength.

During the following centuries, it underwent a number of alterations, especially at the beginning of the 19th century, when Napoleon Bonaparte was threatening to invade England, and later during World War II. But since its initial capture in the 11th century, the castle has never been taken by a foreign invader, and its medieval keep has stood proudly over the Strait of Dover, an immensely strong key of England.

lORDS and VASSALS

A S LONG AS I SHALL LIVE, I AM BOUND TO SERVE you and respect you." In the Middle Ages, intense personal vows such as this one – which is so alien to modern ways of thinking – were uttered by men during a ceremony that bound them in service as vassals to powerful noblemen.

The ceremony, known as the act of homage, was performed with great solemnity: the man knelt down with his hands clasped by his prospective lord, or *seigneur*, who then kissed him and raised him to his feet. Following this, the vassal swore an oath of fealty on the Bible or a holy relic that he would "love what his lord loved and loathe what he loathed" and would be a loyal servant for both his and his lord's lifetime.

The personal relationship created between the two men carried rights and obligations on both sides, and it formed the basis of a strongly hierarchical type of society which later historians have called "feudal." However, feudalism was never a planned or coherent system uniform throughout Europe: it differed according to the region, and some areas, such as Scandinavia, were barely touched by it at all.

Feudal ties have roots that go back to the time when the Roman Empire was disintegrating in the fifth century A.D. (pp.8–9). As it became increasingly battered by waves of German tribes, such as the Goths, Franks, and Vandals, many citizens in the provinces sought the protection of powerful noblemen in return for personal service. The conquering German tribes also had their own tradition of personal loyalty in the relationship between the *comitatus*, the "war companions," and their tribal war leaders.

From both these Roman and German customs, feudal practices began to emerge in northern France between the 8th and 10th centuries. During this time, the powers of the Carolingian rulers (pp.10–11) were in decline, and savage raids by Scandinavian Vikings spurred nobles into seeking greater physical security by making grants of land, or

⚜ tHE SEAL *of the English king Henry II (1154–89) authenticated charters on his behalf. In an age of increased bureaucracy, the royal seal was a system by which the king's will was made known.*

benefices – for money was scarce – to free fighting men in return for military service. In time, the nobles and their vassals formed a military cadre of mounted armored knights and a social elite. Its classic, most centralized form was established in England by William of Normandy in the 11th century.

Noblemen with vassals frequently paid homage to even more powerful magnates than themselves; and they, in turn, would often commend themselves to a prince or king. Thus, in some parts of western Europe, a loose pyramid of relationships came into being, with the king or local prince – in theory, at least – at the apex. Below him were nobles, such as dukes, counts (or earls, their equivalent, in England), and barons. And dependent on them for land and protection were the knights and their servants, or esquires.

But a relatively ordered hierarchy, as imposed in England by William the

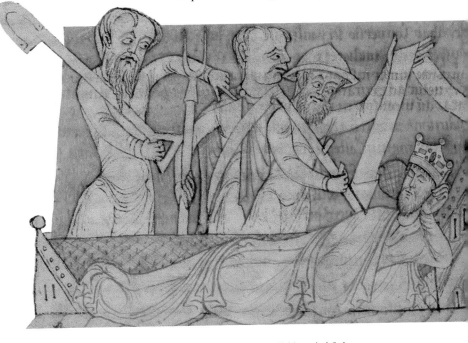

⚜ aNGRY pEASANTS *(above left), brandishing pitchfork, scythe, and spade, and fully armed knights (above right) bear down menacingly on the sleeping King Henry I of England (1100–35). The scenes are part of a famous dream experienced by the king in which he is beset by the three estates*

✤ tHE CRUCIFORM
Saxon church of St. Mary (above) lies to the south of the keep, with the first century A.D. Roman pharos, or lighthouse, standing partially ruined beside it. When St. Mary's was built during the 10th century for the use of the castle's garrison, the pharos was incorporated into the overall structure as a free-standing bell tower.

✤ rOUNDED ARCHES,
carved with zigzag chevron ornamentation, and foliated capitals atop cylindrical columns lend an austere but striking beauty to the entrance of the lower chapel in the keep. Senior household members held services in this single-roomed chapel, which is illuminated by light from its two windows; the king and the constable used a three-roomed chapel above.

Conqueror, was the exception; and even there, when royal control was weak, as in the reign of King Stephen (1135–54), anarchy and the illegal seizure of castles were symptomatic of a malfunctioning political and social structure. And the widespread use of paid troops and of fees in money rather than land further disturbed any perfect feudal pattern.

A lord expected his vassal to attend his court of law, muster knights in time of war, and give counsel and money, often in substantial amounts – for example, to pay the lord's ransom if he was captured in battle. Other more bizarre services have also been recorded: one English vassal's duty was to hold the king's head whenever he crossed the English Channel in a boat. In return for his services, a vassal received not only a unit of land, or fief, but also military and judicial protection from his feudal superior.

The church was partly inside and partly outside these arrangements. In theory its lands were held in inalienable ownership; but in

⚜ THE PRINCE OF WALES, Edward of Lancaster (1453–71), an exile from England, bends on one knee to clasp the hand of the French king, Charles VII, in an act of homage. By this ceremony, common in the Middle Ages, two men were bound together in a relationship that entailed reciprocal obligations.

of feudal society – knights, clergy, and peasants. As the son of the Norman William the Conqueror, Henry was particularly concerned with strengthening his position as king of England, although the incident illustrates the anxiety felt by all those at the top of the hierarchy to maintain the order of society.

practical terms in England, abbots and bishops were treated as feudal lords, bound by certain duties and services. Nor were the services rendered purely spiritual: in 1356 three French bishops fought against the English army at Poitiers, and the archbishop of Sens was killed fighting the same enemy at Agincourt in 1415 – all in defiance of canon law.

Feudal arrangements became established in varying degrees in Germany, Spain, and northern Italy as well as in England and France. From the 13th century onward, the growth of centralized monarchies and the increasing influence of the towns undermined the power of local lords. At the same time, armies raised by the enlistment of vassals were being replaced by strong bands of mercenary troops. But these changes were gradual, and elements of a feudal-like system persisted in Germany until the middle of the 19th century and in Russia until the revolution in 1917.

The ᴀʀᴛꜱ *of* ᴋɴɪɢʜᴛʜᴏᴏᴅ

CLAD IN PLATES OF GLEAMING ARMOR AND CARRYING a sword and shield emblazoned with a lion or other heraldic device, the knight is one of the most potent symbols of the Middle Ages. This was especially so during the Gothic revival in Europe in the 19th century, when enthusiasm for all things medieval rekindled an interest in tales of King Arthur and the legend of the Holy Grail, whose heroes, such as Lancelot and Galahad, were paragons of medieval knighthood.

In reality, however, the knight was a professional warrior, whose heavy weapons and thick armor made him a one-man equivalent of the modern tank. All knights were freemen, but they were not necessarily the sons of freemen.

A knight would often start his career at the tender age of seven, when he served his father as a page. Later, he would join a different noble household, where he would receive instruction in martial arts. In time, he was deemed to be ready to go to war as a shield bearer, or esquire, for his lord.

Only when an esquire was well versed in fighting and could afford the necessary expensive equipment was he ready to become a fully fledged knight. The initiation ceremony, or dubbing, was often held on a battlefield and consisted of a knight touching the shoulder of the esquire with the flat blade of a sword.

Knighthood gradually became associated with a code of behavior known as chivalry – a word ultimately derived from *chevalier*, the French for knight. Chivalry involved being loyal to one's commanders or feudal superiors and gentle toward humanity, yet brave in battle. It was also interwoven with Christianity. Knights were expected to respect the church and defend the faith. In return, the clergy said special prayers for soldiers fighting pagan or infidel armies, such as those on Crusade in the Holy Land, and blessed their banners before battles.

One of the ways in which knights kept their muscles and sinews strong and their fighting instincts well honed during periods of peace was by competing in tournaments. Said to have been invented by a Frenchman, Geoffroy de Preuilly, who died in 1066, tournaments at first resembled battles, except that opponents were captured and ransomed rather than killed. But by the 14th century, tournaments had been scaled down and had become ritual affairs that were centered on the joust, a single combat fought between two knights, either on horseback or on foot.

With their pageantry and color, banquets and dances, tournaments took on the atmosphere of a carnival, with all the associated trappings. And they drew the full gamut of medieval characters, from armorers, harness makers, and horse dealers to moneylenders, fortunetellers, and prostitutes. Nor was the joust itself always entirely serious: in Acre in Palestine a burlesque tournament took place in 1286, with jousting knights dressed up as ladies and nuns.

The grand tradition of medieval knighthood began to wane in the 14th and 15th centuries. The decline of the Crusades, the increasing success of foot soldiers – particularly archers – against mounted knights, and the development of artillery all took their toll. By the 16th century, knighthood had been reduced from a way of life and code of practice for the flower of medieval youth to an honorific status that monarchs could bestow on whomever they pleased. But, in Chaucer's words, the "verray parfit gentil knight" remains as a vivid symbol of the medieval world which he so vigorously dominated.

⚜ **ʜᴇʀᴀʟᴅɪᴄ ꜱʏᴍʙᴏʟꜱ** *such as this griffin were emblazoned on knights' shields to emphasize noble ancestry and to aid recognition in the heat of battle.*

⚜ **ᴛᴡᴏ ᴋɴɪɢʜᴛꜱ** *joust in a tournament in this detail from a 14th-century Venetian manuscript. Aristocratic jousting, on horseback or on foot, could take place with a number of different weapons, such as swords or lances. The intention was to inflict non-fatal injuries on an opponent, leading to his surrender.*

⚜ **ᴛᴏᴜʀɴᴀᴍᴇɴᴛꜱ** *were as much occasions for flamboyant show as displays of martial arts. In this 15th-century French manuscript illumination (right), knights on horseback holding their standards line up in front of the noblemen and women of the court, seated in boxes, before the start of the festivities.*

COURTLY LOVE

*a*NDREAS CAPELLANUS, believed to have been a chaplain at the court of Marie, countess of Champagne, wrote a treatise *c.*1185 on the art of courtly love in which he summed up this medieval concept. He said true love must be free, mutual, secret, and noble. The lover would eat and sleep little; and should he meet his lady in public, he must treat her as a stranger. He concluded that this love could "have no place between husband and wife."

Courtly love was an idealized code of behavior practiced between noblemen and women. In essence, the lover was expected to address his lady with words of adoration normally reserved for saints. In return, he hoped for her attentions – referred to as the "gift of mercy." Yet, even if this were not granted, he still loved her with the same ardent passion. Inspired by his lady, the lover sought to be brave in tournaments or battles, to be gentle in her presence, to defend her honor, and to celebrate her in song.

The origins of courtly love are obscure, although many scholars trace it back to the Moorish culture of Islamic Spain. Moorish poets wrote of a mystical doctrine of love as a sacred passion, pure and elevating; and of lovers who, though parted, remained faithful and devoted.

This Moorish literature fed into the traditions of the poet musicians, or troubadours, of the courts of southern France, whose songs celebrated the cult of true love. Troubadour songs spread to Italy and northern Europe, in the process suffusing some of the great literature of medieval Europe, such as Guillaume de Lorris' *Roman de la Rose* (a scene from which is shown left) and Geoffrey Chaucer's *Troilus and Creseide.*

✤ WOMEN GATHER IN HAY *on the left bank of the Seine River opposite Paris, in a page from the Duc de Berry's* Très Riches Heures *(15th century).*

TOWN AND COUNTRY

" The only pests of London
are the immoderate drinking of fools
and the frequency of fires. "

Medieval chronicler William Fitz-Stephen, 1173

THE CENTURIES AFTER THE FALL OF the Roman Empire in the fifth century A.D. were a time of urban decline in western Europe. But from the 11th century onward, a period of peace after the destructive raids of the Norsemen of Scandinavia, relative political stability, and an increase in population led to a revival of town life. Old Roman towns, such as Cologne and Florence, revived, and new ones were founded – often at key points on trade routes. For urban renewal went hand in hand with the expansion of commerce, in which the cities of northern Italy took a lead in overseas trade with the Muslim cities of the Middle East.

Increased trade and wealth in Europe promoted the production of goods, which in turn stimulated the economy and accelerated the growth of towns. Civic buildings began to rival cathedrals in splendor. And, with the rise of the first universities in the late 13th century, towns also became centers of learning and education.

At the same time, life in the country remained much the same as it had been in the past and would continue to be for a long time in the future. In much of Europe, life revolved around the lord's manor, which typically consisted of a village, arable fields, forest, and common land. The rhythms of the seasons dictated the lives of peasants, whose main aim was to produce enough food to survive.

Although country life was improved by better farming techniques, such as the use of the heavy-wheeled plow pulled by horses, the lot of the peasant was hard. The possibility of drought, crop blight, and famine could never be discounted. And even worse was the threat of epidemics such as the Black Death, which from 1347 to 1351 devastated Europe, killing about 20 million people.

gROWTH of tOWNS

*I*T CONTAINS SO MANY BEAUTIFULLY BUILT CHURCHES and palaces! So many marvelous things can be seen in the streets or courts! Of the abundance of wealth – gold, silver, every type of robe, and holy relics – it would be tedious to tell...." The reaction of the Frankish crusader Fulcher of Chartres to Constantinople on his arrival there in 1097 was one of sheer awe. There was nothing in western Europe to compare with the Byzantine capital – nor indeed with the great Muslim cities of Damascus, Baghdad, and Cairo in the Middle East.

Yet, during the 11th and 12th centuries, towns began to grow in number and size in western Europe, transforming the shape of society in the Middle Ages. Their rise can be attributed to various factors: a period of peace after the depredations of the Vikings and other warrior peoples and an increase in population – itself partly due to an improvement in agricultural techniques (pp.56–57), food production, and diet.

Relative political and social stability stimulated trade (pp.58–59). And as rich merchants began to set up permanent warehouses and offices in towns, the increased wealth and demand for products revitalized old settlements and created new ones. Greater opportunities for work lured large numbers of peasants – both free and unfree – from the countryside, as well as peddlers, small traders, and vagrants.

Some towns grew up on sites naturally suited to trading – along the banks of rivers, on coasts, or at crossroads. Others, such as Cologne and Milan, emerged from the doldrums of their ancient Roman settlements in new guises. Yet others owed their existence or expansion to a castle, monastery, or holy shrine. Santiago de Compostela in northern Spain, for example, grew as a result of being a popular pilgrimage shrine.

As towns increased in size, their leading citizens – often members of guilds (*opposite*) – sought to govern themselves and so effectively place themselves outside the obligations of feudal society (pp.36–37). This naturally led to conflict with the authorities – kings, clergy, and noblemen – who held the land on which the towns were sited. Eventually, leading citizens of a town sought to buy a charter which allowed them to form a commune, which would give them the right to self-government, as well as the right to formulate laws, mint money, carry arms, and levy taxes. And although nobles might have resented the towns' aspirations toward autonomy, they themselves benefited from the tolls and taxes they imposed and the goods and services the towns supplied.

Freedom from the hierarchical authority of feudal society was reflected in a greater sense of equality within the town walls. Unfree peasants, or serfs, for example, were often allowed to become free citizens provided they had lived in the town for a year and a day. The contemporary German saying *Stadtluft macht frei*, "town air makes you free," was no empty boast.

Nevertheless, conflicts of authority still occurred. In 1112, the bishop of Laon tried to suppress the town's commune. In order to do so, he had to buy the king's permission; and to recoup his money, he, in turn, tried to impose a severe tax on the town. The result was a riot. A lynch mob found the bishop quaking in a wine barrel and butchered him.

As towns prospered, new walls, moats, gateways, and impressive civic buildings were manifestations of wealth translated into stone. In Italy, buildings such as the Palazzo Vecchio in Florence and the Palazzo Comunale in Siena

♣ **THE FORTIFIED HILL TOWN** *of Carcassonne, France, commands a natural vantage point on the Aude River's right bank. A settlement since Roman times, Carcassonne grew in medieval times under Louis IX (1226–70) and his son Philip III. The crenellated ramparts that enclose the town's narrow medieval streets first date from this period.*

CRAFT GUILDS

One of the most important institutions of medieval urban life, the guild was an association of merchants or craftsmen and retailers that regulated work practices and gave its members social and financial support. In many towns, guilds were so prestigious that membership was crucial for participation in the town's governing body.

Craft guilds, which included weavers, dyers, cutlers, clothiers, bakers, butchers, carpenters (shown above in a 15th-century French illustration), and cabinetmakers, regulated work procedures, wages, and hours of work, and supervised the training of apprentices and the quality and price of goods and products. The members also protected their own livelihoods by restricting membership.

Guild members met in guildhalls and had their own altars, chaplains, and side chapels in churches.

They gave financial support to members who were sick or old, and to the widows and orphans of those who had died. On holy days they might arrange entertainment for the townspeople with religious "mystery plays" in the marketplace or on stages set up on carts that could be drawn to various venues within the town.

The members of guilds were usually divided into three classes. Those who were considered fully qualified by their respective guilds were known as master craftsmen. Apprentices could spend between two and seven years without pay learning their craft and usually lived with their masters. After they had learned some skills, they became journeymen, which meant they could work by the day for wages. In time, when they had saved up enough money and, in some guilds, passed a final test, journeymen set up business as masters.

asserted a secular challenge to religious architecture. Walls and gates protected the citizens from external threats and helped to regulate traffic and the collection of tolls. And plots of land, where fruit and vegetables could be grown, were common within the walls.

The focal point of a typical town was the market square where the principal church, bell tower, and town hall stood. Narrow winding streets, smelling of decomposing refuse, led off from the center. There was rarely a municipal garbage removal system, and human waste was usually just poured outside the house. Indeed, Louis IX of France (1226–70) is said to have been showered with the contents of a chamber pot while walking along a street. Houses were generally narrow, airless, and gloomy inside. In northern Europe they were often built of wood and were consequently vulnerable to fire – a hazard increased by the use of straw mattresses and open hearths.

The rate and nature of urban expansion varied according to the region. In southern Europe, where the remains and traditions of the Roman Empire were stronger, urban growth was concentrated on the older settlements. In southern France, for example, Nîmes, a Roman town whose population had dwindled to the extent that its citizens lived within the confines of its amphitheater, began to expand with the growth of trade in the Rhône Valley. And in northeastern Italy, Venice, built on islands north of the Po estuary, became powerful and dominant through commercial activities in the eastern Mediterranean.

In northern Europe, where the Roman influence was less enduring, numbers of new towns were founded – still evident from names such as Newton and Villeneuve. The Flemish towns of Ghent, Bruges, and Ypres all prospered through the manufacture of cloth. In Germany, the Bavarian city of Nuremberg was founded in 1040 on the Pegnitz River. This commanding position allowed it to grow as a result of the commerce that passed through from northern Europe to the Alpine passes in the south.

In the west, the future great cities of London and Paris began to expand. Paris became the capital of France during the time of the Capetian kings (987–1328). Its position on a fertile plain beside the Seine River and at the junction of north–south trade routes made it a strong commercial center, and its population increased to 100,000 – larger than that of any other northern city.

The reinvigoration of town life marked a shift in medieval society away from the manorial institutions and practices predominant in the countryside. The greater sense of freedom is summed up by the Jewish traveler who, after his visit to Italian towns in the 1160s, wrote admiringly: "They have neither kings nor princes to govern them, but only judges appointed by themselves."

A new class of urban citizens, known as burghers, burgesses, or bourgeoisie, stood outside the traditional categories of nobility, clergy, and peasantry. Towns became centers of specialized skills and wealth, and provided the right conditions for universities to flourish.

❧ **the narrow lanes** *of Sigüenza in central Spain are of a typically medieval pattern, winding around the town's fortified church which stands in the background. A church or marketplace usually provided the only open space in a crowded medieval town, a relief from the dense clusters of insanitary streets.*

Modern Florence, sprawling northward from the Arno River almost to the Tuscan hills, is shown in the photograph (*previous page*). The dome of the cathedral, or duomo, dominates the center of the picture, with Giotto's campanile, or bell tower, to the west. Just behind it, the dome of San Lorenzo, the Medici family church, is visible. In front of the cathedral rises the square tower of the Palazzo Vecchio, the medieval seat of government.

The same landmarks are shown in this reconstruction – as they were in the 15th century, when Florence was a fair-sized walled town. The greatest of Florence's many festivals is in progress – the feast day of Saint John the Baptist, celebrated on June 24. Making their way across fields and bridges, Florentines stream through the narrow streets toward the Baptistry Square (to the left of the cathedral). The river is traversed by its four medieval bridges, including, second from the right, the Ponte Vecchio with the shops which ran along its length. Open fields inside the walls have been left by the planners to accommodate further development. Indeed, the city only began to outgrow its medieval walls in the 19th century.

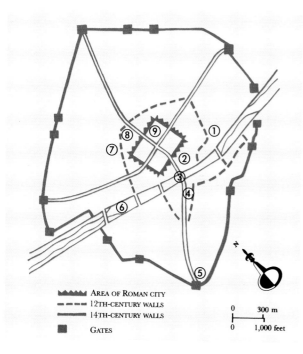

AREA OF ROMAN CITY
12TH-CENTURY WALLS
14TH-CENTURY WALLS
GATES

0   300 m
0   1,000 feet

♣ STAGES OF fLORENCE'S dEVELOPMENT, *with the main east–west and north–south roads indicated, are shown in this plan. The most important medieval sites are:* **1** *Santa Croce* **2** *Palazzo Vecchio* **3** *Ponte Vecchio* **4** *Pitti Palace* **5** *Porta Romana* **6** *Arno River* **7** *Santa Maria Novella* **8** *San Lorenzo* **9** *Duomo, campanile, and baptistry*

Straddling the Arno River in Tuscany, the city of Florence grew in the 13th century to become one of the great commercial and banking centers of Europe. The city's wealth and architectural splendor were such that one contemporary citizen hailed it as the "flower of Italy and its fairest part."

Florence was founded in 59 B.C. by the Roman general and statesman Julius Caesar on the ruins of an earlier settlement. From the sixth century A.D., it began to expand rapidly under first Byzantine, and then Carolingian, rule. By the 10th century, it was an important ecclesiastical center, and the baptistry, which stands outside the cathedral and where mass baptisms were performed twice a year, dates from this time.

In 1115, Florence's leading citizens threw off the shackles of the counts of Tuscany and ruled in the name of the people. In the early 1200s, the first craft guilds were set up, and by the end of the century they dominated the governing council. By this time, two rival political factions, the Ghibellines and the Guelphs, had come to prominence in the city. Ghibellines favored the Holy Roman Emperor, Guelphs the pope, and the struggle between the two groups rumbled on for generations.

Trade was encouraged by the city's advantageous position on the Arno, which made it easily accessible from the port of Pisa. The city's main exports were wool and cloth, and Florentine merchants quickly established themselves in the burgeoning European markets. Their acceptance as the preeminent European bankers and financiers followed, and the Florentine gold florin – first issued in 1252 – became a standard coin throughout Europe.

It was in the 14th century, however, that Florence blossomed fully and its population eventually reached an estimated 100,000. In 1333, new walls were built; these contained the city and its citizens until the 19th century. Many of the older wooden buildings were replaced by stone ones. The Ponte Vecchio (*below*), connecting the two halves of the city, was built over the narrowest part of the river. Shops sprang up along most of its length; but Florentines were especially proud of the space left in the center of the bridge, from which the view could be admired.

By the later part of the 15th century, the city's population had shrunk to about 60,000. But it remained politically important, heading a state encompassing six subject cities, including Pisa and Arezzo. Trade and politics were inextricably linked since, as an independent republic, the Florentine state was governed by members of its 21 guilds, headed by the most prestigious ones – merchants, bankers, lawyers, and skilled craftsmen.

As wealth became increasingly influential in city politics, the real governors were its richest citizens. The Medici family, in particular, came to prominence in the 15th century with the rise of Cosimo and his grandson Lorenzo de' Medici. Under the Medicis, Florence's artistic development, already established by Dante Alighieri and Giotto di Bondone, flowered in the great achievements of the Italian Renaissance.

Seats of Learning

THE ATTITUDE TOWARD LEARNING IN THE MIDDLE Ages is perhaps encapsulated in the words of Bernard, chancellor of Chartres cathedral, who, contrasting the scholars of his own time with the ancients, remarked: "We are dwarfs mounted on the shoulders of giants, so that we can see more and farther than they." Bernard's giants were the early church fathers, in particular Saint Augustine, as well as classical authors such as Virgil, and, together with the biblical scriptures, they constituted the bedrock of medieval learning.

Before the rise of universities in Europe at the end of the 12th and during the 13th century, education was in the hands of the monastic and cathedral schools. Especially important were those in northern France at Chartres and Laon, and in Paris, where Peter Abelard (*opposite*) built his reputation. The schools' curriculum was based on the "seven liberal arts." These were subjects that had developed during antiquity and consisted of two parts: the trivium (grammar, logic, and rhetoric) and the quadrivium (arithmetic, geometry, music, and astronomy).

Various factors contributed to the rise of the universities. First, conditions were made favorable by the growth of towns and a greater exposure to classical learning through commercial contact with the Byzantines in the east. The Muslims in the Norman kingdom of Sicily, those who ruled in Spain, and those in the Middle East, who had absorbed much Greek culture from their Byzantine subjects, were also influential. The translation of the works of the Greek philosopher Aristotle into Latin, for example, did much to stimulate intellectual debate. In particular, it inspired the Dominican friar and theologian Thomas Aquinas to reconcile the rationalist thinking of Aristotle with the Bible and the teachings of the church.

But the direct impetus came when groups of teachers, especially in cathedral towns, banded together into a guild or corporation, known as a universitas. They gave lectures to anyone who could afford the fees and granted degrees, recognized throughout Europe, which were also licenses to teach. From these loose associations, the first important universities, such as Bologna, Paris, and Oxford, arose.

At first, there was little of the infrastructure associated with their modern descendants – no directors, committees, or university buildings. Rules and regulations varied. Students, who could be admitted when they were as young as 12, often lived together in communal houses, and these gave rise to the colleges of Paris and Oxford. In time, universities became renowned for specialist subjects – law at Bologna, theology at Paris – and attracted students from all over Europe.

Universities were established throughout the 13th century – sometimes due to friction between town authorities and teachers, which led to the latter leaving to set themselves up in other places. For instance, Cambridge and Padua were founded in 1209 and 1222 as a result of an exodus of scholars from Oxford and Bologna, respectively.

In other places, church and secular authorities established universities for their own purposes. Pope Gregory IX, for example, founded the one at Toulouse in southern France in 1229 to nurture orthodox doctrine in the face of the heresies of the Albigensians (pp.94–95). And Emperor Frederick II founded one in Naples in 1224 to counteract the pro-papal influence of Bologna. Elsewhere in Europe, universities were founded at Salamanca (*c*.1227) and Valladolid (*c*.1250) in Spain; while in eastern Europe and Germany, Prague (1348), Cracow (1364–97), and Heidelberg (1385) became important seats of learning.

❧ SALAMANCA UNIVERSITY *in Spain has retained many of its medieval buildings and colleges, such as the 15th-century courtyard seen here. From its foundation in the 13th century, Salamanca was one of the principal centers of learning in Europe, with 7,000 students at its peak in the 16th century.*

THE MEDIEVAL TOWER
of Castagna was the original meeting place of Florence's governing body, which later moved to the Palazzo Vecchio. In the Middle Ages, hundreds of similar towers loomed above the surrounding buildings. They were built by rich families in the city, both for defense and for ostentatious effect. During the Guelph and Ghibelline rivalry, opponents' towers became targets for hasty demolition, often causing damage to surrounding buildings. Consequently, a law was passed in 1250 restricting the height of Florence's towers.

LORENZO DE' MEDICI (1449–92) receives a bowed petitioner in this 15th-century illumination. Although he held no official office in Florence, Lorenzo enjoyed the prestige of a sovereign. His encouragement of artists, including Leonardo da Vinci and Michelangelo, helped to foster Florence's cultural flowering in the 15th century.

DANTE ALIGHIERI (1265–1321), Florence's greatest poet, was one of the most influential thinkers of the Middle Ages. In this 15th-century painting, the poet is depicted before Florence's walls holding his greatest work, The Divine Comedy.

PETER ABELARD

*O*ne of the most brilliant medieval theologians, Peter Abelard was born in 1079. An original thinker, he set himself up as a lecturer in Paris and soon had a large, devoted student following.

In 1115, he became tutor to Heloise (shown left with Abelard in a 14th-century manuscript illustration), the young niece of Fulbert, a canon of Notre Dame cathedral. Their ensuing love affair became a *cause célèbre* and resulted in their secret marriage and a son named Astrolabe. But Abelard paid the price for his love: the outraged Fulbert hired thugs to castrate him. Nonetheless, after a year in a monastery, he was lecturing again.

Abelard became involved in more controversy when, in 1121, his teachings on the church's doctrine of the Trinity were condemned by a church council. The following year saw the appearance of his most influential book *Sic et Non* ("Yes and No"), in which he set out excerpts from the Holy Scriptures which appeared to show logical contradictions.

After several years of traveling from place to place, Abelard returned to Paris in about 1136 and enhanced his reputation as a writer and teacher. But it was from this time that he came into conflict with the powerful monastic reformer and mystic Saint Bernard of Clairvaux, who accused him of heretical teachings. As a result, Abelard was brought before the Council of Sens in 1140.

Two years later, he died at the priory of St. Marcel at Chalon-sur-Saône. His remains were transferred to the Convent of the Paraclete where, until her death in 1164, Heloise was abbess.

❧ STUDENTS ATTEND A LECTURE *at Bologna University, Italy, in this 14th-century relief from the tomb of an Italian law professor. Lectures at university began at 6 a.m. or earlier and lasted up to three hours. Teachers would rent a room, read a classic text, then comment on it to the students, who would sit on the floor or, as here, on benches. Although some of the students here have books, parchment was rare and expensive, and it was more usual for students to make mental rather than written notes.*

Another popular method of instruction was by "disputation," in which a student put forward a controversial point of view in his subject field and then defended it against his peers.

BEFORE AND DURING THE RISE OF TOWNS IN medieval Europe, the basic economic and administrative unit in England, northern France, and elsewhere was the manor or, in France, the *seigneurie*. The manor, which was presided over by a lord, varied in size. It typically consisted of a village or villages whose nucleus was formed by the lord's castle or residence, a church, and the houses and hovels of peasants. There were also generally two or three large arable fields, common and waste land, and woodland, all of which belonged to the manor.

Fields were split up into small strips (pp.56–57), some of which were granted to the peasants for cultivation, while the others made up what was called the lord's demesne. To help him with the day-to-day management of this estate, the lord appointed a bailiff, who would also sometimes keep the accounts and, with the help of senior villagers, judge petty crimes.

The manor was generally self-supporting and required few goods from outside – usually only salt, to preserve meat; iron for implements; and luxury goods for the lord. And the community was served by the necessary specialist craftsmen, for instance blacksmiths, potters, millers, and cobblers.

In return for the lord's protection, the peasants were bound to farm his demesne for a specific number of days per week – usually two or three – as well as extra days at sowing and harvest time. Although the peasants were poor, they still had to pay the lord for certain services and permissions. For example, they paid rent for their dwelling places – usually in the form of a pig or a chicken or two; for having their grain ground at the lord's mill; or for marrying a daughter to someone from another manor. In addition to all of this, they had to give a tenth, or tithe, of their produce per year to the parish priest for the support and upkeep of the local church. Moreover, in France, peasants often had to pay *taille*, or tallage. This was an arbitrary tax that was imposed by the lord when he needed to raise money for something specific.

Once the practice of slavery had died out in England in the 12th century, the peasants could be divided into two main groups: villeins, or serfs, who were bound to their land and its lord; and freemen, who were not. A serf could not travel or work where he wished, and he also needed his lord's permission to inherit his father's landholding (in which case, the death duty would often consist of the best head of cattle).

❧ **a lord gives instructions** *to his general manager concerning the grape harvest in this 15th-century depiction of Bruges, Flanders. Industrious peasants are busy hoeing and pruning the vines, while others crush the grapes. In the main building, wine is stored in barrels and tasted. When a lord required extra services from his serfs in peak periods, they might be recompensed with additional food or drink.*

On the other hand, the serf did have certain rights. He had a title to his landholding and was allowed to pass it on to his family. He could graze his cattle on the common land and let his pigs feed on acorns in the forest. Nor was it in the lord's interest to abuse his serfs, since he relied on their sweat and toil to produce the food he and his household lived on.

The contemporary attitude toward the serf was ambivalent. For example, a churchman such as Anselm of Laon wrote: "Servitude is ordained by God, either because of the sins of those who become serfs, or as a trial, in order that those who are thus humbled may be made better." However, a rather more common perception of servitude was probably the one expressed by the 12th-century scholar Gerald of Wales: "There is nothing that so stirs men's hearts and goads them to honorable action like the lightheartedness of liberty; and nothing which so deters and depresses them like the oppression of servitude."

By the 14th century, many lords were seeking money rents from their serfs rather than services in kind, as markets for both land and goods became more cash-based. Granting leases on land became increasingly widespread, particularly after the Black Death wiped out a high proportion of the agricultural workers and raised the day wages and status of those remaining. And numbers of peasants were drawn to towns, many to escape the bonds of servitude by residing within the town walls for the necessary year and a day.

❧ **english peasants,** *wearing coarse woolen smocks, reap grain at harvest time in this illustration from a 13th-century psalter calendar. The standing figure overseeing their labor is either a bailiff or a reeve. In the manorial system, the bailiff was a farm manager who oversaw the work done by peasants, mainly in the lord of the manor's own land, or demesne. He also kept accounts for the lord. Subordinate to the bailiff was the reeve, or foreman, who was sometimes elected by the peasants themselves.*

fARMING *the* fIELDS

MEDIEVAL PEASANTS, AS ONE CONTEMPORARY expressed it, licked the earth, ate the earth, spoke of the earth, and placed all their hopes in the earth. If most peasants were to some degree in servitude to a feudal superior, their relationship with the earth was even more binding: to the earth they owed their existence. The overriding concern of life – beset as it was with the threat of drought, crop blight, and famine – was to produce enough food to survive or eke out a meager existence.

Agriculture, therefore, was the principal concern of the majority of Europe's population, and the pattern of farming varied according to the region, climate, terrain, and soil. In the Mediterranean area, for example, the grape and the olive were the important staples. In northern and western Europe, farming was based, in many areas, around the manorial estate (pp.54–55), and typical crops included wheat, oats, barley, beans, and legumes. Cows, pigs, oxen, sheep, horses, and chickens were also kept and grazed on the common land. Because there was not usually enough hay fodder in the winter, most of the animals were slaughtered in the fall and salted down for future consumption.

Peasants had rights to a number of strips of land – usually marked off by stones – which were scattered among the two or three large fields of the manor. The effect of this was what historians call the open field system, whereby peasants worked in unison and plowed, planted, and harvested at the same time, contributing draft animals and equipment to the common cause.

By the start of the 11th century, farming in northern Europe was benefiting from a number of improved techniques and implements that increased productivity. One important innovation was the heavy-wheeled plow. In the Mediterranean, the light Roman "scratch plow" – effectively just a wooden spike dragged by oxen – was used for the light, dry soils of the area. But this implement was inadequate for the moist clay soils of northern Europe, where

from about the eighth century onward, a new type of plow was introduced.

This heavy "German" plow was built with a colter, or heavy blade, to penetrate the soil and a moldboard to turn the soil over. However, it was expensive, heavy, and required eight oxen to pull it. Only when oxen were replaced by horses – which could cover more ground and work longer – did the plow come into its own. And the increased number of draft horses led to the widespread use of horseshoes and rigid horse collars, which deflected the strain from the neck.

Another effective development was the three-field system. To counteract soil exhaustion – a result of grain

leaching nitrogen from the soil – one field in three was left fallow for a year. So, for example, winter grains, such as rye and wheat, were sown in one field; spring grains, such as oats and barley, in the second; while the third remained fallow. The crops were then rotated after a year.

Advances in technology also included the use of water and wind power. To grind grain into flour by hand was arduous, and mills powered by water wheels were a great blessing to medieval peasants. Water mills had been known in Europe for centuries. They were used by the Romans and, by about A.D. 800, they were common enough in the area that is now France for the emperor Charlemagne to tax them. By 1300, the French town of Rouen possessed a dozen mills, and this was not an uncommon number in other towns in Europe.

From the late 10th century, water-wheel technology was being applied to other processes – for example, operating the bellows of blast furnaces. During the 13th century, mills powered by wind – pioneered by the Muslims in the relatively waterless terrain of the Middle East – were becoming a common sight throughout Europe.

✤ THE HEAVY-WHEELED PLOW, *shown in this 16th-century French illumination (left), was a great advance on the earlier scratch plow, which was ineffective in the clay soils of northern Europe. Another advance was the use of rigid collars on draft horses.*

✤ WATER MILLS *had been in use since Roman times, but were adapted in the Middle Ages for a multitude of purposes, including olive pressing and crushing mash for beer. In this 15th-century French illumination, grain is being carried to the mill to be ground.*

FLESH, FISH, AND FOWL

for the medieval peasant, food was basic, substantial, and usually abundant, except during times of famine. But diet varied according to the region. Italian peasants, for example, lived mostly on beans, raw onions and turnips, garlic, and pasta and bread; while for Germans, cabbage, sauerkraut, lentils, dark bread, and porridge were among the staples.

In England, countrymen fed themselves on beans, peas, wheat or rye bread, cheese, and curds. And French peasants enjoyed stews and soups that they supplemented with bread and washed down with wine or, in the north, cider.

In all regions, eggs, poultry, and pork were common. And noblemen everywhere enjoyed not only the best of peasant fare but also the spoils of hunting – game and venison, for instance – as well as pastries and sweetmeats made with almond paste. In a large manor house, meat pies, pastries, cakes, and bread were baked in wood-burning ovens in the kitchen. Large cuts of meat and poultry, however, were usually roasted on a spit, which was turned by hand over a blazing fire (as shown above in this illustration from a 14th-century English manuscript).

Also common in the medieval diet was fish, which was caught all around the European coastline and transported to markets inland. Particularly popular was salt herring – a principal export of the Baltic regions – as well as cod and mackerel.

Much sought-after spices, which helped to enliven an otherwise bland diet, were imported from India and the East via the Levant. Pepper was common, as were cinnamon, mace, nutmeg, cloves, and ginger.

Perhaps the most important commodity was salt, which was used not only as a flavoring, but also to preserve meat and cure fish. Salt was produced by evaporating sea water – a process that took place at various centers around Europe's seaboard, for example, near the mouth of the Loire River on the Atlantic coast of France.

The *g*ROWTH *of* *t*RADE

*D*URING THE CENTURIES FOLLOWING THE FALL OF the Roman Empire, long-distance trade to and from western Europe atrophied, but never died out. This was despite the fact that the imperial road network had fallen into neglect and, from the seventh century onward, the rise of Islam had turned the Mediterranean into a "Muslim lake."

The revitalization of western commerce was centered around the coastal cities of Italy, which maintained contact with Constantinople, the great Byzantine capital. Situated as it was at the crossroads between Europe and Asia, it had kept its trading links with the East. In 1082, Venice received trade privileges – exemption from taxes – from Constantinople, which helped her expand her trading network throughout the eastern Mediterranean to both Christian and Muslim towns.

Genoa and Pisa – fierce competitors on Italy's western coast – also became prominent, especially during the Crusades (pp.98–100), when, after the Christian conquests in the Holy Land, their citizens took up residence in hostels established in Jerusalem, Acre, and other cities. Damask (from Damascus), muslin (from Mosul), and gauze (from Gaza) are some of the fabrics whose names commemorate their provenance from this time. Italian ships brought back cinnamon, cloves, pepper, and other spices from India, silks from China, and precious gems from Arabia. In return, they exported commodities such as iron, wood, and slaves.

From the cities of Italy and others on the Mediterranean coast, such as Marseilles and Barcelona, various streams of commerce flowed inland. From Venice, for example, caravans laden with goods headed through the Po Valley to the Alpine passes and beyond. Pisa's increased wealth benefited Florence and other towns in Tuscany. And from Marseilles, traders took their mule trains up the Rhône Valley toward Lyons and the north.

In northern Europe, trading centers flourished in the valleys of rivers such as the Rhine and Seine, which saw the expansion of Cologne and Mainz, and Paris and Rouen, respectively. Honey, fish, and furs were typical northern commodities. Wool manufacture was an important industry in the Netherlands where, in the Flemish towns of Ghent, Ypres, and Bruges, weavers worked their looms to make cloth mainly from wool brought over from England. In time, English towns such as Norwich and Winchester developed their own cloth industry and rivaled their counterparts across the water.

In the early Middle Ages, merchants spent most of the year traveling great distances in pursuit of business. Towns were merely bases for storing and then shipping on their goods. However, by the late 13th century, the number of markets had increased significantly, giving merchants greater flexibility. Operations were often controlled from their home town, using professional carriers to transport goods or products overland to markets, where they could be sold or exchanged.

Most famous of these markets were the fairs of Champagne in eastern France, which were held six times a year. These fairs lasted for 49 days and merchants traveling to them enjoyed the protection of the local lords in return for payment. Merchants from England brought bales of wool on the backs of mules; those from Germany came with furs and linen; and Spanish traders arrived with leather goods. The last week of the fair was spent settling accounts; and the moneychangers who gave loans and credits became known as bankers from the benches, or "banks," on which they used to count their coins.

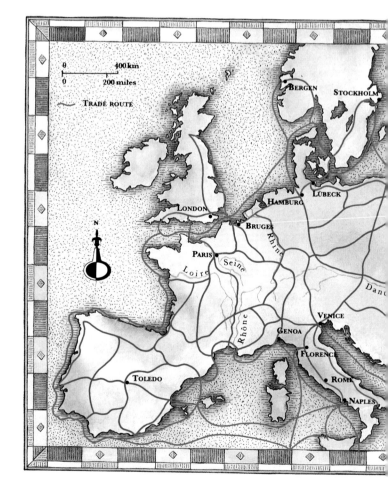

the hanseatic league

a s trade grew throughout Europe, merchants formed associations, or guilds (pp.42–44), and towns sometimes formed trading alliances to protect their commercial interests. The greatest alliance was that created in northern Germany and known as the Hanseatic League (from *Hanse*, "association").

Led by the ports of Lübeck and Hamburg, the Hanse towns dominated Baltic trade. In this 15th-century illumination of Hamburg (*left*), merchants stand on the quay side while barrels are unloaded by wooden cranes from their ships. The three figures under the arch to the right are customs officials, waiting to inspect the goods.

The Hanse towns combated piracy on the seas; helped to improve navigation by training pilots and building lighthouses; and established trading centers and monopolies. The League was at its most powerful in the late 14th century, when it had more than 70 associated towns as well as important commercial enclaves at London, Bruges, Bergen, and Novgorod.

Hanse towns came to monopolize the trading of Russian furs for Flemish cloth, the fish trade of Norway and, after the defeat of King Waldemar IV of Denmark in the mid-14th century, of the entire Baltic. To ensure its commercial preeminence, the League resorted to boycotts and trade embargoes to pressurize obstinate towns and kings.

✤ the principal routes *of European trade are shown on this map, along with the most important market towns. Where possible, trade routes followed rivers to and from ports. Towns such as Toledo in Spain developed where trading routes intersected. Italy dominated commerce with the East, while Hanse towns led by Hamburg and Lübeck dominated trade in the Baltic region.*

✤ a deal is struck *by traders in the Gulf of Cambay, on the western coast of India, in this 15th-century French manuscript illumination. Europe traded items such as iron and wood with the East, gaining in return spices from India, fabrics from the Middle East, and silks from China.*

The GREAT DYING

WHEN A MERCHANT SHIP FROM THE CRIMEA sailed into the port of Messina in Sicily one day in October 1347, it caused a grim sensation. The oarsmen were literally dying at their stations, and the decomposing bodies of the rest of the crew and passengers were strewn around them on the decks. When the Messinans were lifting the corpses off the vessel, they noticed that the bodies had large black swellings in their armpits and groins. It was the ominous coloration of these lumps that would later give rise to the name of the Middle Ages' most deadly plague: the Black Death.

Known at the time as the Great Dying, the plague struck Europe like a dark whirlwind from 1347 to about 1351. For four years, the disease, which seemed like the vengeance of God, ravaged the continent, particularly the towns, whose narrow streets, poor and overcrowded housing, and insanitary conditions helped to spread it. The cause of the plague was a bacillus, identified

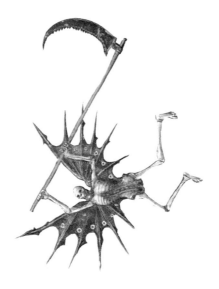

✦ THE ANGEL OF DEATH *wielding his deadly scythe was a potent symbol in the Middle Ages, and fear of the plague led to a morbid fascination with death.*

in the 19th century as *Pasturella pestis*, which thrived in the bloodstream of the small black rat, *Rattus rattus*, as well as in the fleas that lived on the rat. The plague originated in central Asia and initially made its way westward via the caravan routes. But since the rats thrived on ships, the deadly bacillus soon spread along the Mediterranean coast and up vessel-bearing rivers into the heart of Europe.

From Sicily, the plague reached northern Italy within weeks. From there, it passed by ship to Marseilles, southern France, in early 1348. It then moved north to Normandy and England. By late 1349, Britain and northern Europe were groaning under the effects of the disease.

The bacillus entered humans in either of two ways: directly into the bloodstream or via respiration. Apart from the black swellings, or buboes, other symptoms included delirium, vomiting, suppurating lesions, and a high fever, which could last for a week before the victim succumbed. The dead were carted off and usually dumped

in communal pits. But the sheer number of corpses meant that they were frequently left to rot in the streets.

About 20 million people died in Europe in just four years, reducing the total population by about a third. Cities were struck hard. In Paris, for example, the death rate climbed to about 800 mortalities a day. And yet anomalies occurred. In Italy, Florence was decimated, but nearby Milan was barely affected. Bohemia in central Europe also escaped.

Although there were later outbreaks of the plague, the Black Death had largely run its course by the end of 1351. Its long-term effects were dramatic, and not always for the worse. With the working population greatly reduced, peasants suddenly found themselves able to demand higher wages and better conditions. Eventually, however, this led to the enforcement of wage limitations, which in turn exacerbated social tensions.

In various parts of Europe, organized protests broke out. Of these, the two most famous were the Jacquerie in France in 1358 and the Peasants' Revolt in England in 1381. Both failed, and the political status quo in each country was more or less restored. But the terrible plague brought about great long-term social changes and indelibly impressed itself on medieval literature, painting, and religious attitudes, which at times showed an almost obsessive fascination with death.

♣ POPE GREGORY THE GREAT *appeals to heaven to rid the city of Rome of plague – brought back from the East – in this manuscript illumination from the* Très Riches Heures *of the* Duc de Berry. *In spite of the pope's prayers, a monk and a young boy have collapsed from the disease behind his back. Although this depiction shows an event that occurred in 590, its execution in the 15th century would certainly have been influenced by similar scenes of death and supplication during the time the Black Death ravaged the continent of Europe.*

HELL OR PARADISE?

*t*he Black Death and the common occurrence of people dying before their time had a profound effect on the imagination of medieval artists. It also focused people's minds on the idea of the Last Judgment – the moment at the end of time when the dead were believed to rise again and be judged by the Son of God.

Notions of what happened to a person after death developed through the Middle Ages. Church murals, frescoes, and mosaics would typically depict scenes of Christ sitting in majesty, with the souls of the blessed to his right enjoying paradise, while on his left yawned the mouth of hell and a bottomless pit. Below his feet the dead would rise from their tombs. Sometimes they would be shown climbing up a ladder to heaven, or falling from it into vats of boiling liquid or into the mouths of devils, as shown in this detail from a vision of hell by the medieval Italian artist Fra Angelico.

The idea of a place or state known as purgatory, where the dead would be purged of their sins by the heat of fire or the rigors of cold before they could go to paradise, was a powerful doctrine. Saint Bernard of Clairvaux (1090–1154) summed it up: in paradise, the blessed would receive a vision of God; in hell, the wicked suffered eternal torment; in purgatory, the dead were purified and had the hope of salvation.

If people did penance on earth, it was believed they would lessen their suffering in purgatory, and this made fasting, practicing austerities, and going on pilgrimages popular. From the 12th century, it was possible to buy "indulgences" from the church which could replace such penance. But it was a recipe for abuse, and the church's reputation suffered. By the early 1500s, a German monk named Martin Luther was citing sales of indulgences as evidence of a corrupt church. The Reformation had begun.

ARCHITECTS AND STONEMASONS *employed in raising a new church are inspired by a priest's words in this 15th-century illumination.*

HOUSES OF GOD

" Make me a Sanctuary so that I can reside among them. "

Moses instructed by the Lord (Exodus 25:8)

DURING THE MIDDLE AGES, EUROPE echoed to the sound of stone being cut and carved as masons and other craftsmen raised churches and cathedrals all over the continent. Between 1050 and 1400, some 80 cathedrals and 500 churches were constructed in France alone.

In the early medieval period, the predominant architectural style was Romanesque, characterized by round arches, thick walls, and stylized, often abstract sculpture. During the 12th century, it was superseded by a new style. This was termed Gothic by a 16th-century Italian, Giorgio Vasari, who saw in it the barbaric taste of the Goths, the German tribe that had hastened the downfall of Rome.

Today, however, the Gothic style is seen as the crowning glory of medieval building. Cathedrals such as those at Amiens in France and Cologne in Germany are gravity-defying miracles of space and light, filled with clusters of pillars, acres of glass, pointed arches, and ribbed vaulting.

The interiors of churches and cathedrals were veritable caverns of artistic works that not only pleased the eye, but also instructed the mind. Stained glass, sculptures, wooden screens, frescoes, and murals all portrayed scenes from Christian scripture and history. Other eye-catching objects were reliquaries – chests or boxes, often gilded and gem-encrusted, which held holy relics that attracted pilgrims from all over Europe.

But if the church could express its spirituality in its magnificent houses of God, its manifestation through human agents often left much to be desired. In the 14th and 15th centuries, for example, the status of the papacy was diminished with the moving of the papal capital from Rome to Avignon in France, followed by a schism in which two rival popes were elected. And in the latter part of the 15th century, the papacy's reputation declined further with a succession of Italian popes who were remembered more for their corruption than for their piety.

dREAMING SPIRES

FOR THE NOBLES AND PEASANTS of western Europe, the church provided a spiritual framework for everyday life. It also held out the promise of a life beyond the grave – a hope dramatically rendered in stone in the form of churches and cathedrals whose soaring spires lifted the heart and spirit toward heaven and whose interiors revealed a sacred world of color and wonder.

The church was organized into areas known as dioceses – which were under the control of bishops – subdivided into archdeaconries, rural deaneries, and then parishes served by local priests. The bishop usually had his "seat," or *cathedra*, in the principal church, or cathedral, of the most important town in the diocese. To help him administrate and take services, he had a staff consisting of a dean and other clerics who formed the cathedral "chapter."

Cathedrals were objects of civic pride and the focal point of towns: Amiens cathedral in France, for example, was so large it could hold almost all of the town's population of 10,000. They were also catalysts of social unity: during the building of Chartres, the local people harnessed themselves to wagons to bring the stones to site. And Milan cathedral benefited not only from generous donations from the local duke, but also from gifts of grain, poultry, and other humble commodities given by the poorer citizens.

More than simply a house of God, a cathedral was also used for secular affairs. Its size made it ideal for local commercial transactions and fairs. Wine merchants, traders, trinket sellers, town officials, and peddlers could all be found at various times in the nave and outer parts of the

◢ A ROMANESQUE TYMPANUM, *or semicircular relief panel, above the main doorway of the cathedral at Trogir, Croatia, depicts Christ's nativity. The portal is flanked by figures of Adam and Eve.*

building – the choir area and altar were reserved for the clergy only.

Church architectural styles developed during the Middle Ages from the Romanesque to the Gothic. Romanesque architecture was strongly influenced by ancient Roman buildings – as well as by Byzantine, Islamic, and Celtic art forms – and reached its peak in the course of the 11th and early 12th centuries. It was characterized by rounded arches and doors, solid masonry, and an emphasis on horizontal, not vertical, lines, and had local variations all over Europe. Churches were typically cruciform and many, especially pilgrim churches such as that of St. Martin at Tours in France, had at their eastern ends a number of radiating chapels where displayed relics could be reached by a semicircular walkway.

Another Romanesque feature was the barrel vault – a semicircular masonry roof – and the cross or groin vault, formed from the intersection of two barrel vaults. The outward and downward thrust exerted by these vaults required thick walls and massive piers or columns to support them. This in turn created an effect of solid, if gloomy, grandeur.

From the middle of the 12th century, however, the Gothic style emerged, embodying a greater freedom of spirit and a commitment to elegance, lightness, and height. Sometimes this ambition overreached itself, as in the case of Beauvais cathedral in France, whose choir was raised nearly 160 feet (50 m) – before it collapsed.

The great innovation of Gothic building was the creation of vaults out of intersecting stone ribs between

which thin stone panels were laid. This reduction in the amount of masonry diminished the downward and outward thrust so walls could be made thinner and, in addition, could be broken up with large glass windows. Pointed arches replaced round ones and helped to distribute the weight of the downward thrust. At the same time, walls were bolstered on the outside by semi-arches known as flying buttresses and could be raised much higher than before.

The building of a cathedral was under the supervision of a master mason who, like an architect, drew his ground plans and elevations on slabs of plaster or wooden boards. The master mason had under him an army of workmen – both skilled and unskilled – including carpenters, metalworkers, glaziers, painters, and manual workers. Most respected of all were the masons, who cut and positioned the blocks of stone and carved stone sculptures, ribs for vaulting, and traceries, or ribwork, for windows.

Stone, sometimes already roughly cut into blocks, was brought to the site from quarries by unskilled workers and lifted into place with pulleys and cranes. For the vaults, stones were cut for the ribs and cemented onto a wooden framework known as centering. The area between the ribs was then filled with cut stone and, when the mortar had set, the centering was taken down and used again.

The epicenter of the Gothic style was the Ile-de-France – the area around Paris – and particularly the abbey church of St. Denis, which was begun in the late 1130s under the guidance of Abbot Suger (pp.66–68). From here, it spread to other parts of Europe where, over the years, national variations gradually became evident. In Italy, for example, where the light is strong, windows tended to be smaller and Gothic buildings were often less monumental in scale. And in southern Spain, Moorish influence was still powerful – as shown in the style of Seville cathedral, whose bell tower was once the minaret of a mosque.

teams of masons *carve blocks of stone while others mix mortar in this 15th-century French illumination showing a Gothic cathedral being built. In the Middle Ages, entire communities were involved in this enterprise.*

the soaring height *of Amiens cathedral typifies 13th-century French Gothic architecture. A seemingly endless vertical line was achieved by the innovative use of pointed arches, slender columns, and ribbed ceiling vaulting.*

ɪNTERIOR ɡLORIES

⚜ ᴛʜᴇ ꜰʟᴀᴍɪɴɢ ᴊᴇᴡᴇʟʀʏ
of medieval stained glass provided vivid visual narratives for a largely illiterate population. This early 13th-century window from Chartres cathedral, France, depicts scenes from the life of Saint Lupin, bishop of Chartres in the sixth century. The glass was a gift from the wine merchants' guild. The public donation of stained-glass windows by the tradesmen of cathedral towns was both a show of prestige and a form of advertising.

⚜ ʙɪʀᴅs ᴀɴᴅ ꜰɪsʜ
adorn this column capital from the 12th-century Romanesque cloisters of the monastery of Moissac, France. Column capitals provided the medieval sculptor with an opportunity to craft infinite variations on the themes of biblical events and scenes from the lives of the saints. This prompted Bernard of Clairvaux and others to condemn what they considered unnecessary and distracting ornamentation.

"I AM A POOR IGNORANT WOMAN; I CANNOT READ. Inside my village church I see Paradise painted… and Hell, where the damned are boiled. One frightens me, the other gives me joy." With these lines, the 15th-century French poet François Villon let a character speak for the illiterate masses of medieval Europe for whom the images found inside churches and cathedrals were like pictorial sermons. As they looked around them, they could see looming out of walls, screens, and stained-glass windows the figures of Jesus Christ, the Virgin Mary, and the saints, together with biblical scenes from the Creation to the Last Judgment, and vivid depictions of heaven and hell.

Art for art's sake was a concept that was totally alien to the medieval mind. Artistic endeavor was the hand-maiden of its mistress, the church, and had the function of teaching points of theology, morals, and discipline and elevating the mind. Even the structure of churches, with their cross-shaped plans, symbolized Jesus' crucifixion: his head was represented by the chancel at the east end, his arms by the transepts, and his body by the nave.

During the 11th century, as Europe began, in the words of a contemporary chronicler, to "clothe itself in a white robe of churches," the need for artists and craftsmen to create sacred art increased. Not everyone, however, was impressed by the effects of art. The influential Cistercian monk, Saint Bernard of Clairvaux, for example, writing to a French abbot, complained that richly carved column capitals were a distraction from God: "In short, so many and so marvelous are the varieties of divers shapes on every hand, that we are more tempted to read in the marble than in our books, and to spend the whole day in wondering at these things rather than in meditating the law of God."

But if Bernard epitomized a puritanical love of austerity and simplicity – embodied in the starkness of early Cistercian architecture – the other end of the spectrum was represented by Abbot Suger of St. Denis (1081–1151). In his writings on the building of the abbey church, Suger expressed his passionate belief that colored glass, glistening metals, glittering jewels, and other light-reflecting objects had the effect of leading the mind to God. An inscription in St. Denis summed up Suger's doctrine: "The dull mind rises to truth through that which is material and, in seeing this light, is resurrected from its former submersion."

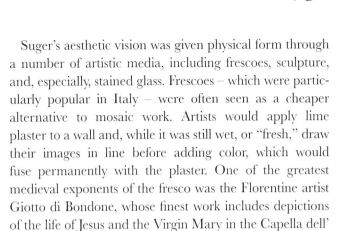

Suger's aesthetic vision was given physical form through a number of artistic media, including frescoes, sculpture, and, especially, stained glass. Frescoes – which were particularly popular in Italy – were often seen as a cheaper alternative to mosaic work. Artists would apply lime plaster to a wall and, while it was still wet, or "fresh," draw their images in line before adding color, which would fuse permanently with the plaster. One of the greatest medieval exponents of the fresco was the Florentine artist Giotto di Bondone, whose finest work includes depictions of the life of Jesus and the Virgin Mary in the Capella dell' Arena in Padua.

The craft of the sculptor extended to column capitals, friezes, and corbels, which were skillfully decorated with foliage, birds, beasts, abstract forms, and human figures. Romanesque sculpture is best exemplified in semicircular panels known as tympana. Set over church portals and richly carved with typically solemn and stylized figures, these tympana depict important Christian themes, such as the damnation of the wicked, the ascension of Jesus, or Christ sitting in majesty.

Gothic sculpture, by contrast, put more emphasis on freestanding, more realistic figures, with expressive faces and flowing draperies. Tomb sculpture was also popular in the Gothic period and, from the 14th century, death masks were used to render faithful likenesses of the deceased.

ABBOT SUGER

a key figure in the development of Gothic architecture and an influential patron of the arts, Abbot Suger was born in 1081 into a peasant family. His humble birth, however, was no bar to his becoming the secretary of Adam, abbot of St. Denis near Paris, and adviser to both kings Louis VI and Louis VII. Indeed, when Louis VII went on the Second Crusade in 1147, he made Suger regent of France, a responsibility to which

Suger rose. His duties even extended to passing laws and suppressing a revolt by French nobles.

In 1122, Suger became abbot of St. Denis and set about improving the fabric of the place as well as instilling a greater sense of purpose into an institution that had become, in the words of one hostile contemporary, "the synagogue of Satan." In the late 1130s, Suger began to rebuild the abbey church and is believed to have been the

guiding hand behind the various architectural features that together heralded the start of the Gothic style: ribbed vaulting, the pointed arch, and large quantities of stained glass.

And inside, the great cross and reliquaries which he had encrusted with emeralds, topaz, sapphires, and other gems embodied his ideal: "The work should brighten minds so that they might travel . . . to the True Light where Christ is the true door."

The most dramatic realization of Suger's aesthetics, however, was stained glass, whose widespread appearance coincided with the rise of Gothic architecture in the 12th century. Stained glass was created by adding certain chemicals, such as manganese and cobalt, to glass while it was in its molten state. The glass was then spun or blown into a sheet and allowed to cool. Shapes were cut out with a diamond point and details, such as faces and draperies, were added in black paint. Individual pieces were edged with strips of lead and soldered together to make larger panels.

Favored colors were reds and blues and, later, browns and greens. Also popular were slightly tinted glass panels known as *grisailles*. In the 14th century, a silver compound was discovered which, when added to glass and fired, produced colors ranging from pale yellow to deep orange. It was used for details such as hair and haloes, which could now be made on one piece of glass rather than having to be leaded in separately.

The best stained glass was created in France and some of the finest examples can be seen at Chartres cathedral and the Sainte Chapelle in Paris. Chartres was rebuilt starting in 1194 after a fire and was endowed with more than 100 stained-glass windows. Many depict the Virgin Mary – to whom the cathedral is dedicated – while others show the individuals and trade guilds that paid for them. A scene of Noah building the Ark, for example, echoes the craft of the carpenters, coopers, and wheelwrights who donated the window. The shafts of polychromatic sunlight shining through the windows, together with the marble columns, created such a luxuriant effect that local people called the cathedral interior *la fôret*, "the forest."

The Sainte Chapelle, the royal chapel of Louis IX, was built to house the relics of a fragment of the crucifix and a piece of the crown of thorns. Glazed between 1244 and 1248, it contains more than 1,000 panels depicting biblical scenes. Some are bordered by heraldic emblems, such as the lily of France, and together they create the effect of hanging Persian carpets made of colored ice – legend says that when Henry III of England saw the chapel, he immediately wanted to take it back to his realm on a cart.

CARVED AND PAINTED FIGURES *of Adam and Eve adorn a rood screen (above) in St. Fiacre church, France. These screens, which divided the choir from the nave, provided medieval artists with the opportunity for creating elaborate carvings and paintings.*

WINGED DEMONS *flee the Italian town of Arezzo, expelled by Saint Francis of Assisi, in a fresco by Giotto di Bondone (c.1267–1337). This great Florentine painter's achievement was to depict religious scenes with a greater naturalism than had previously been seen in Gothic art.*

Soaring majestically from the west bank of the Rhine River, Cologne cathedral, or the Dom, is the largest Gothic church in northern Europe. In the Middle Ages, pilgrims traveled here from all over Europe to marvel at its great structure and to venerate the relics of the Magi – the three wise men who, according to the Gospel of Saint Matthew, had come from the East to attend the birth of Jesus.

The city of Cologne was originally founded as a Roman settlement in about 38 B.C. But its importance as a Christian center dates to A.D. 795, when the Frankish king Charlemagne – soon to be Holy Roman Emperor – raised the city to an archbishopric. The first cathedral was founded in the following century. But it was only in 1164 that it became a major pilgrimage shrine, when it received the holy relics of the Magi.

The relics were said to have been brought back from the Holy Land to Constantinople by the empress Helena (*c*.285–337), mother of the Roman emperor Constantine. They were transferred to Milan in the sixth century, and there they remained until 1164. In this year, the German emperor Frederick I, Barbarossa, captured Milan and sent the relics to Cologne, where they were later placed in a magnificent shrine made of gold and silver.

In 1248, after the cathedral had caught fire and burned down, a new, much grander structure was proposed to provide the Magi's shrine with a worthy setting and to accommodate the increasing numbers of visitors. The architect in charge, Master Gerhard, was probably present at and inspired by the building of Amiens cathedral in France, whose great height was achieved by the use of ribbed ceiling vaults and flying buttresses.

Cologne's choir, with its seven radiating chapels, each glowing with stained-glass windows, was completed in 1320 and consecrated two years later. Its ambulatory, or semicircular walkway, was made exceptionally large to provide space for the crowds of pilgrims who would file behind the huge marble altar to see the shrine of the Magi. Eleven years later, in 1331, when the Italian poet Petrarch visited the unfinished cathedral, he praised it as "the finest in the world"; yet progress on it was slow.

Work on the Dom ceased in 1560 when the expense proved too much for the city coffers to bear. For 300 years it remained an awesome fragment made up of the choir at the east end, the south tower, and the lower stages of the nave. In the first half of the 19th century, the British poet Thomas Hood described the unfinished building as "a broken promise to God." But in 1888, the promise was kept when, with strict adherence to the medieval plans, the Dom was finally completed.

To be a PILGRIM

THROUGHOUT THE MIDDLE AGES, THE ROADS AND tracks of Europe were alive with pilgrims, equipped with staffs, hats, and water bottles, making their way toward shrines housing holy relics. The reasons for their pilgrimages varied. Some went as a penance for wrongdoing in the belief that their time in purgatory after death would be reduced. Some traveled in the hope that the relic might effect a physical healing; or to give thanks for good fortune. And for others, the pilgrimage was simply an excuse to travel abroad.

The practice of pilgrimage was bound up with the cult of relics – the mortal remains of, or objects associated with, the holy figures of Christianity – and dates back to at least A.D. 156. In this year, Saint Polycarp, bishop of the Roman province of Smyrna, was martyred, and his bones were afterward said to be more precious than "refined gold."

In time, Christians saw the whole of Palestine – blessed by the footsteps of Jesus himself – almost as a relic. An account of a pilgrimage to Jerusalem by a Spanish nun named Etheria in about A.D. 400 shows that by this date local guides were used to showing travelers around sacred sites and that several pilgrim hostels were already well established.

Europe also could boast many holy places, especially Rome, where the bones of saints Peter and Paul were venerated. Eventually, relics came to play an indispensable part in the founding of churches. Pope Gregory the Great (590–604), for example, sent "relics of the holy apostles and martyrs" to Saint Augustine to help him on his missions in England. And in 787, a church council at Nicaea ordered that all new churches should be consecrated with a relic. As a result, the demand for them nearly outstripped supply.

The situation was helped by the traffic of relics from Palestine – especially during the Crusades – as well as by the "miraculous self-multiplication" of others. One pilgrim, for example, is said to have seen the head of John the Baptist at two different shrines. At the second, he was told by an ingenious monk that the first head belonged to John as a young man, while their own was that of John in his later years.

Elsewhere in Europe, alleged splinters of the true cross, Jesus' crown of thorns, entire bodies of saints, the bones of the Magi, and numerous other holy objects were found. And drops of the Virgin Mary's milk were widely sold. As one contemporary remarked: "All the buffalo cows of Lombardy would not have as much milk as is shown about the world."

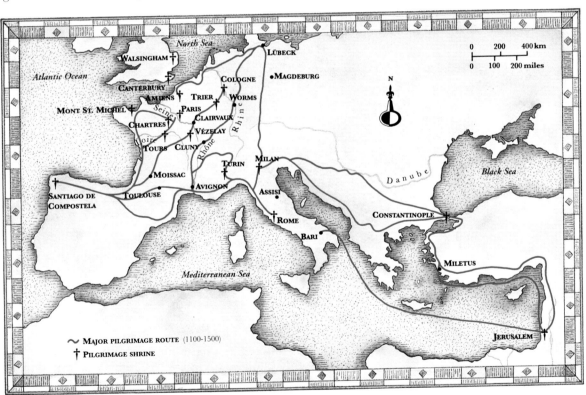

THE PRINCIPAL PILGRIMAGE ROUTES *of medieval Europe and farther abroad are shown on this map. Pilgrims visited relics such as Thomas Becket's bones at Canterbury,* the bones of saints Peter and Paul at Rome, as well as the church of Haghia Sophia in Constantinople and the traditional site of Jesus' crucifixion in Jerusalem.

THE **G**ERO **C**RUCIFIX, *at 6 feet (1.8 m) tall, is one of the largest wooden crucifixes in the Western world. Made from oak in about 975 and named for a local archbishop, it hangs just beyond the north transept, before the first chapel. The letters INRI above Jesus' head stand for the Latin words meaning Jesus of Nazareth, King of the Jews.*

THE **A**DORATION **O**F **T**HE **M**AGI, *painted by local artist Stephen Lochner, was commissioned in the mid-15th century for one of the chapels. The central panel shows the enthroned figure of the Blessed Virgin wearing a golden crown and holding the Christ Child. Around them, in coats of red and green, the Magi offer their gifts.*

🐾 **the romanesque chapel** *of San Miguel in Castile, Spain, provided accommodation for pilgrims on the road to the shrine of Saint James at Santiago de Compostela. The medieval routes to the shrine were dotted with chapels, hostels, and priories.*

After Rome, the greatest European pilgrimage shrines were Canterbury in England and Santiago de Compostela in Spain. The cathedral of Santiago, begun in 1078, claimed to house the remains of the apostle Saint James (*Iago* in Spanish). Christians from all over Europe made the pilgrimage to the shrine by one of four principal routes leading from France over the Pyrenees into Spain. They would have traveled on foot, if poor; on horseback, if rich; or on a litter, if infirm. Each night they would stop at a hostel, which provided basic accommodation and food, or sleep under the stars. Eventually, footsore and weary, they would see the cathedral of Santiago rising before them in the distance.

Once they had arrived and entered the sanctuary, pilgrims headed for the altar and the holy relics. Then they might pick up a scallop shell – Saint James's symbol – or buy a lead badge of one to sew to their hats or clothing, before returning home, refreshed and invigorated, and perhaps confident that their time in purgatory had been reduced.

the Canterbury poet

One of the great poets writing in English, Geoffrey Chaucer was the author of *The Canterbury Tales*, a 17,000-line poem describing the journey of a group of pilgrims from London to the shrine of Thomas Becket in Canterbury. In 1170, the murder of Becket, archbishop of Canterbury, made the cathedral one of Europe's great shrines, attracting large numbers of pilgrims, such as those shown in this 15th-century English manuscript illustration.

Born in about 1340, the son of a rich London wine-seller, Chaucer became a page in the household of the duke of Clarence, the third son of Edward III. He fought in the Hundred Years' War and was captured near Rheims in 1359, but was later set free. From 1370 to 1378 he was sent by Edward on diplomatic missions to Europe and later became a London customs inspector and a justice of the peace. He wrote accomplished and sophisticated poetic works for the royal court, including *Troilus and Creseide* and *The Parliament of Fowls*.

In the 1390s, the last decade of his life, Chaucer embarked on his masterpiece, *The Canterbury Tales*. His literary pilgrims pass the time by telling each other stories – some bawdy and humorous, others moralistic – which form the heart of the poem. He conveys fascinating insights into 14th-century life, with allusions to religion, medicine, astrology, love, and marriage. And his powers of characterization bring to life the pilgrims themselves, from the much-married Wife of Bath to the gentle Knight.

The DECLINE of the PAPACY

WHILE THE SIGHT OF CATHEDRAL SPIRES RISING all over Europe during the 14th and 15th centuries seemed to proclaim the power of the church, the reputation and power of the papacy – the highest office in Christendom – grew more fragile. Part of the reason for this lay in the growing confidence of nation states, such as France and England, to whom papal interference in their domestic affairs was increasingly unacceptable.

In the early 14th century, for example, an explosive clash of wills occurred between King Philip IV of France and Pope Boniface VIII over the trial of a French bishop and the general issue of papal authority. Their quarrel came to a climax in 1302 when Boniface issued a bull, *Unam Sanctam*, reaffirming in the strongest terms the supremacy of the pope over secular rulers. Philip retaliated by sending an armed band to Italy to capture the pope and force his resignation. The aged Boniface escaped, but died soon after. However, the very fact that for the first time a king had dared to take such action was symptomatic of the diminution of papal status.

Then, in 1305, the papacy suffered another blow when the pro-French faction in the college of cardinals – the body of churchmen who elected popes – chose a Frenchman, Clement V, as the new incumbent. Pressured by the French king, in 1309 Clement moved his residence from Rome, the traditional papal capital, to Avignon in southern France. For almost 70 years, a succession of French popes – perceived as being favorable to the

◄ **POPE BONIFACE VIII** *(1294–1303) presides over his cardinals in this medieval illumination. From his pontificate onward, the papal monarchy underwent major attacks from the emergent monarchies of western Europe, particularly Philip IV of France.*

◄ **THE PAPAL PALACE** *stands fortresslike above the town of Avignon, southern France. Between 1309 and 1377, a period known as the Babylonian Captivity, a succession of French popes resided here in opposition to what they saw as Rome's traditional self-interest.*

interests of France – remained in what was called Babylonian Captivity, a reference to the time when, according to the Second Book of Kings in the Bible, the Jews were exiled in Babylon.

The papacy returned to Rome in 1377 with Gregory XI. But after his death the following year, it again fell into crisis. When the newly elected Urban VI showed undue hostility toward the cardinals, a group of them withdrew their support and elected another man, Robert of Geneva, as Clement VII in his stead. But when Urban stood his ground, Clement moved back to Avignon and so initiated the Great Schism, a division right at the very top of the church hierarchy.

Each pope attracted his own supporters: Clement had the backing of France, Spain, and Scotland, while Urban could count on Germany, England, and Hungary. Even when Urban and Clement both died, their successors continued the schism. Theologians and clergy all over Europe were scandalized, and this prompted the rise of the conciliar movement, which was based on the principle that general councils had greater authority than the pope. However, the council that met in Pisa in 1409 only made the situation worse. For although it deposed both popes and elected a new one, Alexander V, the Avignon and Roman popes refused to acknowledge him, and Christendom was in possession of three pontiffs.

The issue was finally resolved at the Council of Constance (1414–18), whose main purpose was to end the schism by removing all three popes and electing a new one.

The council was successful, and Martin V emerged as the sole leader of the church.

But the years of intrigue, infighting, and corruption had taken their toll. The contemporary Italian poet Boccaccio told a story about a Jew who came to Rome and embraced Christianity on the basis that any religion that could survive such iniquities of its leaders must be the true faith. At a more serious level, the papal saga stirred the anger of an eminent, freethinking English theologian, John Wycliffe (c.1330–84), who began to voice his opposition to papal authority.

Wycliffe believed that the Bible, not the pope, was the highest religious authority and that the clergy should not stand above civil law. He also denied the doctrine of transubstantiation – that during the Mass the wine and bread actually change into Christ's blood and body – and criticized church wealth, the cult of relics, and other practices. Wycliffe's views reached as far as Prague, where they gripped the mind of the priest and university lecturer John Huss (1374–1415).

Huss, like Wycliffe, stressed the central importance of the Bible and condemned the corruptness of the clergy and the sale of indulgences, by means of which people could buy salvation and escape the punishment of purgatory. Summoned to the Council of Constance to defend his beliefs, Huss was condemned as a heretic and burned at the stake – despite promises of safe conduct.

Wycliffe and Huss had fired warning shots across the bows of Catholic orthodoxy. But the church failed to address the grievances articulated by both men – a failure that was to "reap the whirlwind" in the early 16th century.

Meanwhile, in the latter part of the 15th century, the papacy remained in the hands of Italians, who held Italy's local and factional interests at heart and who seemed to revel in power, wealth, intrigue, and nepotism. Typical of these so-called Renaissance popes was Rodrigo Borgia, a cunning, immoral, and well-connected man whose election as Alexander VI in 1492 was secured by bribery. Thus, as the new century dawned, the conditions were ripe for a German monk named Martin Luther to transform his repugnance at the church's laxity into a movement that would rock Europe and split the church in two: the Protestant Reformation.

the Czech reformer John Huss first became aware of the theories of the English thinker John Wycliffe when he was a lecturer at Prague University. His outspoken criticism of church power led to his execution in 1415 by burning at the stake.

❡ Pope Gregory the Great (590–604), *shown consecrating the host in this 15th-century illumination, greatly influenced the growth of monasticism.*

THE SECLUDED LIFE

*" Whoever you are, renounce your own will,
and take up the strong and bright weapons
of obedience. "*

From the *Rule* of Saint Benedict

MEDIEVAL MONASTERIES, OFTEN BUILT far from other human habitations in woods or beside mountains, were secluded microcosms where monks retreated from the world and devoted themselves to the life of the spirit. From the 9th to the 13th centuries, thousands of monasteries were founded all over western Europe.

Monks maintained a constant round of prayer and praise of God, kept the fires of scholarship and artistic endeavor burning, and turned wildernesses into miniature Edens. They copied the sacred texts of the Bible and early church fathers, as well as the works of classical authors, and decorated them with illuminations. And they trained men who would become inspiring theologians, teachers, diplomats, and patrons of religious art.

By the ninth century, most monasteries in western Europe followed a guide to monastic life known as the *Rule* of Saint Benedict, written by a sixth-century Italian monk who stressed a balanced life of prayer, study, and manual work. But as monasteries grew in both number and size, they became increasingly drawn into the affairs of the secular world and lost much of their spiritual dynamism. In response to this situation, a number of reforming orders arose, the most successful of which were the Cistercians, founded in the late 11th century.

By the end of the 12th century, however, monasticism had lost its drive and momentum, and it was left to orders of mendicant, or begging, monks known as friars to inject new blood into the church. Most famous of these were the Franciscans, founded by Francis of Assisi, and the Dominicans, the Black Friars, whose intellectual training made them ideal combatants to carry the church's fight against heretical movements.

MONKS *and* MONASTERIES

THE ROOTS OF CHRISTIAN MONASTICISM GO back to the fourth century A.D., when numbers of ascetics retired to the deserts of Egypt. Here, following the lead of Saint Anthony, they lived a solitary or "eremitical" life devoted to God. Some of these hermits – Saint Simeon, for example, who is said to have lived on top of a pillar for 33 years – pushed themselves to the limits of physical endurance. Others, however, influenced by Saint Pachomius, preferred to live a "cenobitical" life (from Greek *koinos*, "common") in organized communities with other monks.

This cenobitical tradition spread to western Europe where, from the fifth century onward, from Italy to Ireland, monasteries were founded in increasing numbers. Each house followed one of a number of rules, or guides, to monastic life; but these were gradually superseded by the *Rule* written by Saint Benedict of Nursia (*c.*480–547), especially after Emperor Louis the Pious made it the standard model in the Carolingian Empire in 817.

In his *Rule*, Benedict stressed the cardinal virtues of obedience, poverty, and humility. Monks were to live together and submit themselves totally to an elected head, or abbot, since they "are men who can claim no dominion even over their own bodies or wills." The appeal of Benedict's *Rule* was its moderation – the saint himself, on one occasion, is said to have upbraided a hermit who had chained himself to a rock with the words "Let the chain of Christ, not an iron chain, hold you."

⏹ THE ABBEY OF RIEVAULX, *with its immense 13th-century Gothic choir (above), was the spiritual center of the Cistercian mission in northern England. The order's devotion to humility is reflected in the austere Romanesque cloister of the monastery of Le Thoronet, southern France (left).*

⏹ GUADALUPE ABBEY'S *late 14th-century grandeur (right) is an embodiment of the Spanish concept of a conjoined monastery and palace where even kings could live the monk's life for short periods.*

farming duties to lay brothers, or *conversi* – illiterate peasants who lived in the monastery complex subject to monastic discipline.

Western monastic life suffered during the ninth century with the incursions of the Vikings. In the early 10th century, however, monasticism revived, particularly after the founding of the abbey of Cluny (pp.85–91) in southeastern France in 910. And, by the 11th century, monasteries had become powerful institutions, renowned as centers of scholarship and creating magnificent works of religious art. Monks found themselves managing large estates – often given to them by wealthy lords hoping for spiritual intercession in return – and supervising tenants or entertaining the entourages of princes and kings.

But the monasteries' growing wealth and involvement in secular affairs bred a reaction, which resulted in a number of reforming orders; these sought to recapture the simplicity and spiritual freshness of the apostles and the early Christian church. The most dynamic were the Cistercians, founded in 1098 by Abbot Robert of Molesme at Cîteaux (Cistercium in Latin). The driving force behind the White Monks – so-called for the color of their habits – was a return to a strict observance of Benedict's *Rule*: it is said the very first Cistercians rejected everything that was contrary to it, including the use of coats, hoods, underclothes, combs, capes, and bedclothes.

Inspired by abbots Stephen Harding (*d.*1134) and Saint Bernard of Clairvaux (1090–1153), the Cistercian

Although monasteries varied in size and shape, they typically consisted of a church, a cloister, a refectory for eating, a library, a scriptorium for writing, an infirmary for the sick, and the abbot's lodge. The monks' day revolved around eight church services largely devoted to singing psalms and chanting. They rose early and filed into the candlelit church for the service of Vigils, or Matins. This was followed at various times in the day by the services of Lauds, Prime, Terce, Sext, None, Vespers, and Compline.

When they were not engaged in worship, monks might discuss day-to-day business in the chapter house; work in the garden; or read, copy, or illuminate manuscripts. They usually had only one main meal a day, which was eaten in silence while one of the brothers read from a holy text. Food might include fish, bread, cheese, beans, cereals, vegetables, and a measure of wine; meat was not allowed, except for the sick. Although they did some manual labor, orders such as the Cistercians would delegate many

▌ᴍodern ʙenedictine ɴuns *uphold a tradition of monastic seclusion that began in the seventh century under the patronage of Saint Scholastica, sister of Saint Benedict.*

congregation multiplied with astonishing speed – 300 houses were founded in Saint Bernard's lifetime alone. Eventually, however, the Cistercians could not maintain their spiritual ardor, and by the end of the 1100s, some of their houses were becoming as secular as those they had set out to reform.

By the start of the 13th century, the zeal behind the monastic movement had faded, and it was left to new orders of friars to breathe fresh spiritual life into the body of western Christendom. The two most important orders were the Franciscans, founded by Saint Francis of Assisi, and the Dominicans, founded in 1220 by a Spanish cleric named Dominic de Guzman (1170–1221).

The Dominicans differed from the Franciscans by emphasizing the intellectual tradition of the church. Monks were rigorously trained in theology to become the guardians of orthodoxy, a crucial factor in the church's fight to stem the tide of heretical movements (pp.94–95).

SAINT FRANCIS OF ASSISI

*b*orn in 1182, the son of a wealthy wool merchant, Saint Francis of Assisi is revered by Christians as "the most saintly among saints" – a man who radiated love for humanity and the natural world in a Christlike way; in a famous incident, depicted by Giotto (*below*), he even preached to the birds. Francis's spiritual destiny was revealed to him as a young man when, on one occasion, he entered a local church and heard a crucifix utter the words: "Go and repair my house because it is falling into ruin."

The incident began a train of events that culminated in his renunciation of the world at the age of 24. He became a beggar and began to devote his life to the poor and the sick, and to the Order of Minor Brothers, which he founded with the approval of Pope Innocent III in 1210.

Among Francis's earliest followers was a young Assisi noblewoman named Clare, who decided to run away from home and follow him. Francis was impressed by her piety and, in 1212, made her the head of the Poor Clares, an order of Franciscan nuns.

Francis forbade his followers to own property or even to carry money. He expected them to help the poor, preach the word of Christ, and maintain a respect for the clergy. From 1210 onward, Franciscan missions fanned out from Italy all over Europe, reaching England in 1224.

In the same year, Francis, exhausted and nearly blind, received the stigmata, the replication on his body of the wounds of Christ. Then, in 1226, his health finally gave out; he died on October 3 and was canonized two years later.

In the 12th century, the abbey of Cluny in Burgundy, France, was the largest Benedictine monastery in Europe. By this time, its abbots had achieved such an unprecedented level of influence and power that the Council of Rome had declared in 1077 that "among all the abbeys beyond the Alps there shines first and foremost that of Cluny...without a doubt it surpasses all other monasteries, even the most ancient."

Cluny was founded in 910 by William the Pious, duke of Aquitaine, who built a modest church for only 12 monks. He could not have imagined that two centuries later the number would have expanded to more than 300. From its foundation, Cluny's status was unique because it was directly accountable to the pope and therefore not subject to interference from any local bishop or duke.

The monastery began to expand under the 40-year abbacy of Majelus (954–94), during whose time a second and larger church was built. But it was with a succession of highly able and long-lived abbots, including Odilo, Hugh the Great, and Peter the Venerable, that Cluny reached its zenith.

These men set about giving their organizational skills and advice to other monasteries and thereby created what was initially a loose coalition of houses dependent on Cluny. By the mid-11th century, this coalition had become a formal hierarchy of Cluniac abbeys and included Moissac, St. Martin-des-Champs in Paris, and La Charité-sur-Loire. Each abbey was headed by a prior appointed by the abbot of Cluny, to whom the monks swore an oath of allegiance. In this way, Cluny became the capital of a monastic empire that consisted of about 1,500 abbeys and priories scattered over France, England, Spain, Italy, and other parts of Europe.

In accordance with the abbey's growing influence, a third church was built between 1088 and about 1120; it is referred to by historians as Cluny III. Until the 16th century, when St. Peter's church in Rome was rebuilt, Cluny III had the distinction of being the largest church in the Western world. The octagonal bell tower of the surviving south transept – with its smaller bell tower immediately in front – is shown in the background (*below*), rising above more recent structures.

Cluniac monks typically came from noble families and wore distinctive black habits. Manual work, such as building and gardening, was done by lay servants, who had their own quarters near the monastery's workshops and stables. This allowed the monks to follow a liturgical regime that at the time was the strictest in Europe, with as many as eight hours a day spent in church.

ILLUMINATED WORDS

*T*HE MEDIEVAL DICTUM "TWO FINGERS HOLD THE pen, but the whole body toils" indicates the degree of effort the monastic scribe employed in his task of copying manuscripts. Before the advent of printing in the mid-15th century, the only way to transmit written knowledge was by hand. And after the fall of the Roman Empire in the fifth century A.D., it was the monasteries – particularly those that followed the Benedictine *Rule*, which advocated a balance between study, work, and prayer – that provided the time and tranquillity for the lengthy process of book production.

Throughout the medieval period, the larger monasteries usually had libraries and a scriptorium – a room where letters and documents were composed and books copied. The scriptorium was usually cold and lit only by natural light since open fires and candles were too much of a fire hazard. Books were copied on parchment or vellum, the tanned and polished hide of a calf or sheep. Before the copying began, lines were drawn or scored across the writing material as a guide. The scribe would then sit in silence at his desk – perhaps inspired by Saint Bernard of Clairvaux's words: "Every word you write smites the devil" – and painstakingly copy a text that was laid out in front of him.

Copyists wrote in scripts, or book hands, that developed through the ages. One of the most widely used was the Caroline minuscule, whose neat "lower-case" letters were in stark contrast to the upper-case or capital letters used by the Romans a few centuries earlier.

When the scribe had finished the text, it was often passed to an illuminator, who would paint on illustrations or embellish title pages, margins, or single letters with decorative details. The illuminator's colors were made from a binding agent such as gum arabic mixed with a variety of pigments. These included verdigris (a copper acetate) for green; woad and ultramarine for blue; and orpiment (arsenic sulfide) for yellow. A red earth pigment known as rubrica was used for the books' red-ink title and headings – which became known as "rubrics." Paints were

A MAGNIFICENT ILLUMINATED INITIAL *opens the Second Book of Kings in the lavish 12th-century Winchester Bible. These intricately crafted page-length letters provided visual introductions to the theme of each book. The incidents depicted here are, from the top, the prophet Elijah with the Samarian king Ahaziah, and Elijah in his chariot ascending to heaven watched from below by his companion Elisha.*

usually made by the monks, who naturally experimented with color. One monk, for example, was said to have created red by mixing salt, copper, honey, and urine.

The books that were copied and preserved in monasteries constituted the essentials of Western learning. Most important were the Bible and its commentaries, followed by the writings of the early church fathers and theologians such as Augustine, Ambrose, and Jerome. Also important were the works of Greek and Latin authors, such as Virgil and Aristotle, and various treatises on law, medicine, astronomy, and mathematics. To create an illuminated Bible on vellum could require the hides of hundreds of newborn calves or lambs and could take a year or more to produce.

At first, book copying was done mainly by monks. Gradually, however, more and more professional lay scribes were used, especially with the rise of the universities in the 13th century (pp.52–53), which created an increased demand for books. The universities employed people known as stationers to make sure that the demand was met, and regulations were drawn up about the size, content, and price of books. During the 14th and 15th centuries, a revival in interest in the classics and the growth of lay literacy further stimulated manuscript copying, and during this time, books written in the vernacular became more common.

Manuscript copying and illumination began to decline with the development of printing, pioneered by a German goldsmith named Johannes Gutenberg between about 1440 and 1450. Within decades, printing techniques had spread from Germany to the rest of Europe, allowing the commercial production of small, relatively inexpensive books. Italy's great commercial towns produced the first flowering of elegant, scholarly texts, with France taking the lead in the 16th century. The result of these new advances was that while the number of books in western Europe up to the mid-15th century could be counted in the thousands, by the end of the 16th century that number had risen to more than 9 million.

⫷ THE MONASTIC SCRIBE'S CRAFT is shown in this self-portrait by the English monk Eadwine of Christchurch, Canterbury, dated around 1150. Intricate lettering was painstakingly rendered by the monks and then embellished with colored decoration by illuminators. Books written on parchment and vellum were produced by monasteries and universities, and provide one of the most enduring legacies of the medieval period.

⫷ THE SERMONS OF POPE GREGORY THE GREAT are reproduced in a fine late Romanesque German bookhand in this 12th-century manuscript. The wide use of these sermons is attested to by the huge number of editions published throughout the Middle Ages.

hERETICS

IN TURIN IN *1028, A GROUP OF CHRISTIANS WHOSE*
beliefs had caused them to reject the consumption of
meat, abstain from sexual relations with their wives,
and keep up a constant round of prayer were
burned as heretics. Thousands more would be pun-
ished by death, imprisonment, or penances in medieval
western Europe.

The term "heresy" is derived from the Greek word for
"choice," and in its Christian context it became applied to
those who had put forward their own "choice" of religious
opinions against those of the wider church. Heretical
groups existed from the first century A.D., and by the fifth
century, Saint Augustine of Hippo was able to name
almost 90 different heresies.

Until the Middle Ages, heretics tended to be isolated
individuals rather than organized groups. During the 12th
century, however, widespread disillusionment with the
moral laxity of the church in western Europe led to the rise
of various popular movements, such as the Humiliati and
Speronisti, whose preference for austere living and private
devotion, rather than public worship, diminished the role
of the clergy.

Sometimes, however, the line between orthodoxy and
heresy was a fine one. The Franciscans (pp.82–84), for
example, with their strong emphasis on evangelical
poverty, outwardly resembled other movements that had
been branded heretical. But one crucial difference was that
Saint Francis insisted that his followers should respect the
clergy; and the pope, realizing his potential value to the
church, approved his order.

Of all the heretical groups in the Middle Ages, the two
most significant were the Cathars and the Waldenses. The
Cathars (the Pure) believed that the world was in ever-
lasting conflict between good and evil, spirit and flesh.
This led them to reject the idea of Jesus' incarnation and
the resurrection of the body. The material world was the
realm of the devil, and this extended to sexual relations,
which the most zealous Cathars – the *perfecti*, or perfected
ones – rejected outright.

The dualist beliefs of the Cathars ultimately derived from
the ideas of a religious teacher named Mani, who taught in
Mesopotamia during the third century A.D. The Cathars
themselves are thought by modern scholars to have come
to western Europe from Bulgaria in the early 11th century.
They flourished in northern Italy and southern France,
particularly around the town of Albi. With the support of
Raymond, the powerful count of Toulouse, these Cathars,

or Albigenses as they became known, grew to be a major
force, successfully resisting various attempts by the church
to reconvert them by preaching.

In the end, Pope Innocent III launched a crusade to
eradicate the heretics, decreeing that Albigensian proper-
ties could be legitimately seized. Zealous and greedy for
land, the crusaders crushed the Albigenses with sword and
fire in wholesale massacres. Nevertheless, the movement
survived into the 14th century, when it was finally crushed
by the Inquisition.

The Waldenses were the followers of a Lyons merchant,
later known as Peter Valdes, or Waldo, who in about 1175
renounced his way of life as a wealthy businessman.
According to tradition, Valdes had been told the story of
Saint Alexis of Rome, who, on the night after his marriage,

abandoned his wife to become an ascetic. Eventually he returned to Rome – so changed by his austerities that no one recognized him. For the rest of his life, Alexis lived in his parents' home as a hermit. Moved by the example of the saint, Valdes sought the advice of a local clergyman, who responded with the words of Jesus: "Go and sell your possessions and give the money to the poor, and you will have treasure in heaven; then come, follow me" (Matthew 19:21).

So Valdes gave away his worldly belongings, left his wife, sent his daughters to a convent, and became a wandering preacher, attracting followers wherever he went. At first, the papacy approved of the Waldenses – on condition that they gained the consent of local church authorities before they preached in an area. When they failed to do this, the church's attitude changed: in 1184 a papal bull named them as heretics, a judgment re-endorsed by Pope Innocent III in 1215.

Condemned and persecuted, the Poor Men of Lyons nevertheless spread from France to Italy, Spain, Germany, and other parts of Europe, drawing support mostly from peasants, who were impressed by their piety. In time, worn down by repressive measures, their numbers dwindled, and many rejoined the church.

∏ ALBIGENSIAN HERETICS are expelled from the French town of Carcassonne near Albi and Toulouse, the centers of the movement. The Albigensian protest against the corruption of the clergy at the time attracted much popular support, but was violently suppressed after 1209 on the orders of Pope Innocent III.

∏ HERETICS were treated harshly by the medieval church, which set up the Inquisition to track them down. Inquisitors were often drawn from the Dominican order, founded by Saint Dominic, who is shown here presiding over the burning at the stake of two heretics.

THE INQUISITION

*W*ith the rise of Catharism and other heresies in western Europe during the 12th and early 13th centuries, the church began to react more aggressively toward heretics. In 1162–63, Pope Alexander III proposed that instead of waiting for reports of heretics from informers, officials should be sent out to discover them. Some 70 years later, this policy was developed further when, in 1231, Gregory IX issued a bull setting down procedures for how church agents, or "inquisitors," should root out heretics and persuade them to recant: it was the start of the Inquisition.

The papal inquisitors were usually drawn from friars, especially the Dominicans, who were noted for their rigorous intellectual training. They would arrive in a particular area, urging people to come forward and confess their heresies within a period of grace of up to 30 days. Those who did so usually had to do a penance, such as go on a pilgrimage or attend a certain number of masses. Those who did not confess, but who were suspected of heresy, were brought to trial.

At least two witnesses were needed to establish evidence against the accused, who could be cast into prison for a time to loosen their tongues. Then, in 1252, Innocent IV sanctioned the use of torture to extract confessions. Although the accused were allowed to be tortured only once, inquisitors got around this by calling subsequent torture a "continuation" of the first. Punishments for convicted heretics were harsh and included imprisonment, the confiscation of property, or even being handed over to secular authorities to be burned at the stake.

✝ MOUNTED FRENCH KNIGHTS, *under King Charles II, charge into battle in this illumination from the* Grandes Chroniques de France *(1493).*

INTO BATTLE

" He was fitted with a cuirass...whose double layer of mail could be pierced with no lance or javelin....On his head was placed a helmet, resplendent with precious stones. "

John of Marmoutier describing the knighting of Geoffrey of Anjou in 1128

WARFARE WAS ENDEMIC IN MEDIEVAL society. Chronic rivalries and petty feuds between local princes, lords, and towns were common. There were also major military campaigns – the most celebrated and dramatic of which were the Crusades, when the Christian powers of Europe, fired with religious zeal, fought the Muslims of the Middle East for control of the Holy Land.

There were four major Crusades and many less important ventures. Only one – the first – bore significant military success for the Crusaders: the capture of Jerusalem in 1099 and establishment of four Crusader states. Thereafter, the Muslims chipped away at these "islands" of Christianity until the last bastion, Acre, fell in 1291.

Two other major campaigns were those between France and England in the Hundred Years' War and the epic struggle between the Byzantine Empire and the Ottoman Turks.

The roots of the Hundred Years' War lay in the complex feudal relationship between the kings of England and France. After initial English successes, the French eventually found a new resolve and unity, partly through the efforts of the inspirational Joan of Arc.

The Turkish victory at Constantinople in 1453 was a landmark in Western history, since it ended southeastern Europe's political continuity – via the Byzantine Empire – with the Eastern Roman Empire. A vital factor in the Turks' triumph was their use of artillery, marking a new phase in warfare. Castles, with defenses designed to combat armies with catapults and battering rams, were now vulnerable to huge stone missiles fired from cannons.

Similarly, the effect of gunpowder altered armor and weaponry. Plate armor became outmoded against infantry firearms, which superseded the traditional crossbow and longbow.

HOLY WAR

✝ **THE CAPTURE OF ANTIOCH,** *Syria (left), in 1098, after an eight-month siege, was the first major victory for the Christian armies of the First Crusade in their push toward Jerusalem. The besiegers were themselves surrounded by Muslim reinforcements and suffered terrible privations from lack of food and water. But they drew new resolve from such auspicious signs as the reported discovery of the Holy Lance, which pierced Christ's side on the cross, as well as many miraculous sightings of Christ among the troops. Finally, treachery within the city itself meant victory for the Crusaders.*

✝ **THE ULTIMATE GOAL** *of the First Crusade was achieved when Jerusalem fell on July 15, 1099, after a short siege of only 40 days. As this French illumination (right) shows, the resulting pillage was merciless; all Muslims and Jews in the city were brutally massacred, and many of the city's treasures were carried back to Europe by the departing Crusaders.*

ON NOVEMBER 18, 1095, AN EXPECTANT CROWD gathered in the open air at Clermont in southern France – where a church council was being held – to listen to an address by Pope Urban II. The pope's speech turned out to be a landmark in Christian history, for it set in motion a series of campaigns that proved to be among the most remarkable military expeditions ever undertaken at the prompting of the church.

With fiery invective, Urban urged upon his audience the need to retake the Holy Land from the Muslims. As he cataloged the evils heaped upon Christian pilgrims and holy places by the infidel, the crowd rose to his challenge with cries of "Deus volt!" ("God wills it!"), and some began to pin crosses of red cloth onto their tunics as a sign that they had "taken the cross." Those Christians who later set out for the Middle East became known as Crusaders, from *crux*, the Latin word for cross.

In fact, conflict between Christianity and Islam was not a new phenomenon when Urban preached the First Crusade. In Spain and especially Asia Minor, where the Seljuk Turks were expanding westward, militant Islam had already come face to face with an increasingly aggressive Christianity. From 1079, the Seljuks controlled access to Jerusalem – a city that had been in Islamic hands since 638 – and reversed the policy of tolerance that Islamic rulers had hitherto practiced toward Christians on pilgrimage in the Holy Land.

At the same time, the Seljuks were posing a threat to the Byzantine Empire. Alarmed by their capture of the city of Nicaea in 1092, the Byzantine emperor Alexius Comnenus appealed to the West for aid. And the West responded – for a number of different reasons. The first was genuine piety. Jerusalem, and in particular the Church of the Holy Sepulcher, was the most sacred place in Christendom, and for many Christians its liberation was deemed to be worth the privation of a military campaign and the risk of death.

Urban II's promise of full remission of sins – an unprecedented spiritual reward – to all who participated also spurred soldiers on with the belief that death brought with it a guarantee of paradise. On a more material level, the Crusades held out the prospect of land; power – especially to the papacy; and money to the mercenaries, merchants, financiers, and traders who in various ways supported the military enterprise.

In all, there were eight major crusades that are now identified by numbers, of which the first four were the most important. But there were also numerous other unofficial ventures. In France in 1212, for example, a crusade of children led by a 12-year-old boy headed for the Holy Land in vessels provided – with apparent generosity – by two Marseilles shipowners. But the children had been

MILITARY MONKS

*a*t the time of the First Crusade, the prevailing *Zeitgeist* in Europe was one of deep piety allied with militant aggression. It is not surprising, then, that many young male Christians channeled their energies into the newly founded religious military orders, especially the Knights Templar and the Knights Hospitaler.

The Knights Templar, founded in the early 12th century to protect Christian pilgrims traveling to the Holy Land, developed into an elite force committed to fighting anywhere in the defense of Christendom. Led by local commanders who owed obedience to a Grand Master, the Templars grew in power and wealth, and at their height boasted about 20,000 knights.

In the early 14th century, however, rumors – probably substantially false – that the Templars were heretics and blasphemers began to circulate around Europe. In 1307, the order was persecuted by King Philip IV of France – who almost certainly coveted its extensive lands and wealth – and in 1312 it was officially suppressed by the pope.

The Hospitalers, or Knights of St. John, were founded in the late 11th century to care for sick pilgrims in Jerusalem. Like their rivals the Templars, the Hospitalers grew rich from bequests and developed into a crack fighting force. This 15th-century illumination (*right*) shows members of the order attending the Grand Master, each displaying the distinctive eight-pointed cross.

In 1309, 18 years after the loss of the Holy Land, the knights took over Rhodes and controlled it until 1522, when the Ottoman Turks succeeded in besieging the island. Eight years later, they moved their headquarters to Malta, and from here they continued their struggle against the Turks.

✝ LEGENDARY rIVALS *in the Third Crusade (1189–92), the Muslim leader, Saladin (left), and the English king, Richard I (right), displayed a mutual respect for each other's military prowess. On one occasion, it is said, the sultan sent cooling mountain snow to Richard, who lay fever-stricken in his tent during the Christian siege of the walls of Jaffa in Palestine.*

tricked: the unscrupulous captains took them to northern Africa and sold them into slavery.

The First Crusade (1096–99) attained its main objective: the capture of Jerusalem. But the achievement was sullied by the Christians' wholesale massacre of the city's inhabitants – both Muslims and Jews. After they had sated their bloodlust, many of the Crusaders returned to Europe, having achieved their aims. Those who stayed behind helped to carve out four Crusader states based around the cities of Edessa, Antioch, Tripoli, and Jerusalem, for which they are named.

It was not long before these states came under serious Muslim assault. In 1144, an Islamic force captured Edessa and so sparked a call for a renewed invasion: the result was the Second Crusade (1147–49). An army of 50,000 men led by the king of France and the German emperor tried to overturn the Muslim advances – but in vain, and the Crusade ended in failure.

Then in 1187, Saladin – the sultan of Egypt and Syria and one of the legendary figures of the Crusades – captured Jerusalem. The shock waves caused by this event galvanized the West into fresh action. A host, led primarily by the king of England, Richard I, the Lion-Hearted, and King Philip II of France, again tried to recoup Christian losses. But although this Third Crusade (1189–92) enjoyed some military success, in the end it fizzled out with a fragile peace treaty between the two sides. And, much to Christian dismay, the city of Jerusalem remained in Muslim hands.

The leaders of the Fourth Crusade (1202–4) had originally intended to invade Egypt. However, urged on by Venice, the mainly French and Flemish Crusaders were diverted farther north to Constantinople – Venice's great trading rival – and sacked the city. They then placed one of their number on the Byzantine throne and established the Latin Empire of Constantinople, which was to last for more than 60 years.

In popular literature, the Crusades are associated with knights on horseback, sweltering in their armor, as well as the religious military orders (p.99). Less well known are the ordinary foot soldiers, many of whom were pressed into service for the sake of God, the pope, and their manorial lord and who had little commitment to or understanding of the high ideals of Christian geopolitics. They were on Crusade either in the entourage of their feudal masters or in motley bands escaping the poverty of their lives at home, and died in the thousands, some of starvation, others of diseases such as dysentry and cholera – before they ever crossed swords with a Muslim.

The Fourth Crusade was followed by a number of further, unsuccessful expeditions. The fall of the last Crusader stronghold – Acre – to the Muslims in 1291 dealt a major blow to the Crusading movement, as the whole of the Holy Land fell to Islam.

THE FALL OF CONSTANTINOPLE

May 29, 1453, was a day that altered the destiny of the eastern Mediterranean. For, after an epic siege, the Byzantine capital of Constantinople fell to the Ottoman Turks, giving them a permanent foothold on European soil.

For more than a thousand years, Constantinople had been the glittering hub of an empire which, at its height in the sixth century, had stretched from northern Africa to the eastern Mediterranean. By the 1400s, however, most of the empire had fallen, much of it to the Ottomans. Well aware of Constantinople's strategic importance at the cross-roads of Europe and Asia, Sultan Mehmed II had been determined to capture the city, which he called Kizil Elma, the "red apple."

The Turks' siege preparations began at the end of 1452 with a huge encampment outside the northern end of the city's land walls, built by the emperor Theodosius in the fifth century. They had an army of up to 140,000 men as well as more than 60 cannons, including a unique "great cannon." By contrast, the Christian defenders numbered just 8,000 or 9,000 and were armed only with catapults and a few cannons. For the first few weeks, the Turks bombarded the land walls and tried to scale them. But they were continually repulsed, and the defenders repaired the damaged parts each night. Meanwhile, the Ottoman fleet, positioned in the Sea of Marmara, tried – and repeatedly failed – to break the "great chain," a barrier protecting the Christian harbor in the inlet of water known as the Golden Horn. As a result, the sultan daringly dragged 70 ships over land into the Golden Horn, which allowed his engineers to build a pontoon bridge across the harbor.

The final Turkish land assault began before dawn on May 29 to the sound of drums and flutes and with flares lighting the sky. Fighting was fierce, particularly around the crucial St. Romanus Gate – directly opposite the sultan's camp – where the Ottomans concentrated their attacks. However, with the battle still in the balance, the commander-in-chief of the gate, the renowned general Giovanni Giustiniani, was wounded and forced to leave his post. Alarmed by this, many of his troops thought the battle was lost and began deserting their own posts. This gave the Turks their advantage, and 40 or more of their best men scaled the wall. Cries of "the city is taken" soon echoed in the air from the demoralized defenders. In a last desperate attempt to stem the tide, the Byzantine emperor, Constantine XI, threw himself into the battle, but soon lost his life.

By 8 a.m. the city was in Turkish hands. After allowing his men three days of pillaging, the sultan entered the city and rode to the church of Haghia Sophia, where the Christians had held their last forlorn service the previous night. And, now assured of his position in Europe, Mehmed delivered a triumphant prayer to Allah from the Christian altar.

✝ THE TURKS *pummeled the walls of Constantinople with huge cannons, of which the 17-foot (5-m) long Dardanelles Gun shown here is the closest surviving example. It was cast for Sultan Mehmed II in 1464.*

✝ SULTAN MEHMED II *was just 21 years old when he laid siege to Constantinople in 1453. His chief ambition since becoming sultan two years earlier had been to add the Byzantine capital to the Ottoman Empire. He planned the siege meticulously, studying plans of the city and even consulting his astrologers; at the final assault, he rallied his troops from the thick of battle.*

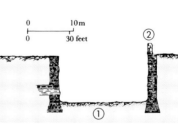

0   10m
0   30 feet

① ② ③ ④

✝ TURKISH GUNS *batter Constantinople in this fresco from a monastery in Romania. The defenders' own guns, shown firing at Turkish ships, were less effective in the siege, since the recoil often damaged the city's walls on which they were mounted.*

✝ CONSTANTINOPLE'S TRIPLE WALLS *are shown in cross section:* **1** *Foss, or moat* **2** *Foss wall* **3** *Outer wall and tower* **4** *Inner wall and tower*

SIEGE WARFARE

*I*N *THE* *MIDDLE* *AGES*, *MILITARY* *SUCCESS* *VERY* *OFTEN* hinged on an army's ability to defend or capture castles and fortified towns. Siege warfare developed throughout the medieval period as improvements in defensive fortifications were matched by advances in siege weapons and techniques.

Assault soldiers often had to overcome a series of obstacles before they could capture a castle. Moats and ditches might hamper their progress up to the outer walls, where protruding towers allowed defending archers and crossbowmen to give flanking fire. From projecting galleries, defenders could rain down projectiles or pour boiling tar, pitch, or water. And within the castle itself, gateways and passages might be guarded by movable grilles, or portcullises. These were lowered to entrap intruding enemy soldiers, who could then be picked off by defenders firing from apertures known as *meurtrières* ("murder holes").

Castles were generally so well fortified that they fell more often than not as a result of starvation, disease, or treachery. The almost impregnable Crusader castle of Krak des Chevaliers, for example, fell only because of a letter forged by its besiegers. Yet an attacking army did have various techniques and machines for winning a siege. Fire was often used to burn wooden structures and to crack stone walls. At the siege of Jerusalem in 1099, the Crusaders wrapped arrows in cotton that was set ablaze and shot them to good effect.

Mining operations were also effective. Soldiers dug tunnels up to the walls, hollowing out a gallery beneath them. They shored this up with wooden beams which were then set alight, collapsing the gallery and – usually – the walls above them.

Stock besieging equipment included scaling ladders, some of which could expand in height like a lattice, while others were of fixed length. But attackers on ladders were exposed to enemy crossfire, and many besiegers resorted to the costly expedient of building movable wooden towers. Known as belfroys or *malvoisins* ("bad neighbors"), these towers rose up four stories and were fitted with drawbridges that could be dropped onto the castle's parapet.

At the siege of Jerusalem, the Crusaders built three great towers and covered them with oxhide to protect them against fire. On the morning of July 15, two of the towers were in place against the walls. From one of them, during a

✝ **t**HE **t**REBUCHET *was used in siege warfare to batter enemy walls. As this French illumination shows, it consisted of a vertical post to which was attached a swinging beam with a missile slung at one end. At the other, a heavy weight flung the missile on a high trajectory, like a modern howitzer.*

✣ bESIEGING sOLDIERS *pick away at the foundations of a castle's walls under the cover of a movable wooden shield in this 14th-century French illumination. Meanwhile, the castle's defenders attempt to destroy the shield by assailing it with heavy stones, wooden stakes, and incendiary materials.*

moment of panic among the defenders, the tower's drawbridge was released onto the top of the wall. In an instant, Christian knights had raced across and secured a position, allowing other soldiers to swarm up on scaling ladders. It was the beginning of the end for the Muslim defenders.

But such towers did have their drawbacks: assault soldiers were crammed into their wooden interiors and risked being roasted alive in fires sparked by incendiary arrows. Also, the ground leading up to the walls had to be leveled or filled in; otherwise, the towers could tilt, grind to a halt, or topple over.

Other besieging weapons included battering rams and a variety of catapults. And while mining or battering operations were in progress, besiegers might keep the defenders occupied with a hail of missiles from such threatening machines as mangonels, trebuchets, and ballistas.

The mangonel was a large catapult that used twisted ropes to create enough torsion to launch a missile from the end of a beam. The missiles were usually large stones; but attackers sometimes engaged in biological warfare by lobbing the rotting corpses of animals into the castle or town. The trebuchet, also a catapult, operated on the seesaw principle and used a counterweight to fling its missiles.

Ballistas resembled giant crossbows. The bolts, stone balls, and javelins they hurled did little damage to masonry, but they were more accurate than the mangonel's missiles and could inflict deadly wounds on personnel.

From the 13th century onward, these siege weapons were gradually supplemented and replaced by artillery. Although the first cannon carried the risk of exploding in the faces of their gunners, they gradually became more effective. During the Hundred Years' War, the Black Prince, son of Edward III of England, used cannons effectively in his assault on the French town of Romorantin in 1356. And the Ottoman Turks employed their guns to devastating effect at the siege of Constantinople in 1453.

The HUNDRED YEARS' WAR

THE DECLINE IN CRUSADING CAMPAIGNS DURING the 13th century was mirrored by a shift in European consciousness away from a concern with the defense of Christendom to a more introspective preoccupation with national identity and the growth of nation states. Symptomatic of this development was the Hundred Years' War, fought between the royal houses of France and England.

This intermittent but protracted struggle rumbled on from 1337 to 1453. Its roots, however, went back to the Norman conquest of England in 1066. From that time, kings of England also had tenure of Normandy in France which made them feudal vassals – and dangerous rivals – of the French king. Between 1154 and 1204, they also held Anjou, Maine, Poitou, and Aquitaine, and thereafter little more than Aquitaine, for which Henry III formally paid homage in 1259.

For the next 70 years, conflicts that arose between France and England were largely resolved by diplomacy and compromise. But in 1328, after the death of the

✠ AMID FIERCE HAND-TO-HAND FIGHTING, *an English soldier leads away two French prisoners during the Battle of Agincourt, in 1415, when a French army was defeated by the English under Henry V. During the battle, which lasted only a day, the numbers of French soldiers taken captive soon outweighed the English troops on the field, and Henry was forced to order them all to be killed despite the loss of ransom that this drastic action entailed.*

French king Charles IV, Edward III of England claimed the French throne, chiefly because his mother was Charles's sister. A French assembly ignored Edward's claim and chose Philip, count of Valois, as king, by virtue of his descent from Charles IV's father in the male line. Edward, however, did not let the matter rest, and by 1337, he was ready to take decisive action: he denounced Philip as a usurper and prepared to prosecute his aims.

In its early stages, the war went well for England. A naval success at Sluys in 1340 was followed by an overwhelming victory at Crécy in 1346. A year later, the English took the port of Calais. Then in 1356, the two sides met at Poitiers in western France. Again the English defeated the French and even captured John II, their king.

Having little to show for his military success, however, Edward made peace with the French in 1360 in the Treaty of Brétigny. By this, Edward renounced his claim to the French throne in return for sovereignty over an enlarged Aquitaine and a ransom of three million livres tournois for the release of John.

But French failure to honor the terms of the treaty led to renewed fighting in 1368. It continued spasmodically for decades and appeared once more to be turning in England's favor when the English longbowmen won a famous victory for Henry V at Agincourt in 1415. Then, two years later, Henry began a major new offensive in Normandy and, crucially, secured the alliance of the duchy of Burgundy, on the eastern borders of France.

When Henry V died in 1422, his purpose was briefly carried on by regents acting for his infant son, Henry VI. Ambition on such a scale was beyond the finances of the English crown, however, and in 1429, Joan of Arc success-fully raised the siege of Orléans. Even more importantly, she persuaded the dauphin, Charles – the heir to the French throne – who had been exiled in Bourges since 1418, to be crowned as king of all France at Rheims.

The decisive turning point in the war eventually came in 1435 when the Burgundians defected to Charles. French recovery thereafter was slow but sure, and in 1453, the English surrendered all their possessions on the continent with the exception of the town of Calais.

The Valois kings had finally triumphed, and the path was cleared for the consolidation of France under a centralizing monarchy based in Paris. For both England and France, national identity had been forged in the crucible of military and political struggle, and both countries emerged with a stronger sense of nationhood.

JOAN OF ARC

*f*rance's greatest national heroine, Joan of Arc, shown here carrying a banner displaying Christ with two angels, was born in 1412 during the Hundred Years' War. As a girl, Joan claimed to hear the voices of saints Michael, Catherine, and Margaret, who exhorted her to go to the aid of Charles, dauphin of France, and fight the English forces laying siege to Orléans.

In 1429, clad in armor, she arrived at the besieged town and, inspiring the French troops with her presence, led them on to victory. She then returned to the dauphin and urged him to go to Rheims to be crowned king, sensing that this would unite the French people in their struggle against the English. On July 17, her efforts were rewarded with his coronation as Charles VII.

A year later, however, Joan's fortunes turned. On May 23, 1430, she was taken prisoner by Burgundian soldiers who sold her to their English allies. Charles, who was making overtures of peace toward the duke of Burgundy, made no attempt to save her.

In 1431, she was tried by an ecclesiastical court on charges of witchcraft and heresy. Despite her fortitude, five months of incessant interrogation by her French and English accusers took their toll: she broke down and signed an abjuration. But a few days later, she retracted it, effectively sealing her death. On May 30, 1431, she was burned at the stake while, at her request, a Dominican friar held up a crucifix and shouted out to her assurances of salvation above the crackle of the flames.

The MEDIEVAL ARMORY

WHEN THE FLOWER OF FRENCH KNIGHTHOOD charged the massed ranks of English infantry at the Battle of Crécy in northern France in 1346, they found themselves up against one of the most potent weapons of the Middle Ages: the longbow. Made of staves of yew or elm and measuring 6 feet (2 m) in length, these bows fired steel-tipped armor-piercing arrows with great accuracy. The effect at Crécy was devastating. More than 1,500 French knights and squires lay crumpled on the battlefield, compared to English losses of only 100 men.

✝ **THE MILITARY SUPERIORITY** *of the longbow over the crossbow is graphically demonstrated in this depiction of the Battle of Crécy. While French crossbowmen had to prime their weapons by laboriously cranking the handle, skilled English archers using longbows were able to fire off 10 deadly arrows a minute.*

gUNS aND gUNPOWDER

*f*rom the 14th century onward, the use of gunpowder, cannons, and handguns brought about a revolution in European warfare. In particular, they showed the fallibility of personal armor and diminished the importance of the castle as a bastion of defense.

The development of gunpowder is usually attributed to Chinese alchemists who, by the ninth century A.D., had discovered that a mixture of saltpeter, charcoal, and potassium exploded on ignition. This "black powder" reached Europe in the 13th century, via either the Mongols or the Arabs. And it was there that its use in weapons evolved.

Early cannons were made of brass or bronze and were as dangerous to the gunners as to the enemy: barrels often blew up or fired their projectiles so inaccurately that soldiers could be killed by "friendly fire." As late as 1460, for example, the Scottish king James II was besieging a castle in Scotland with the help of a huge Flemish cannon known as "The Lion," when it blew up, killing James and all those around him. Handguns developed from the late 14th century and were equally lethal until triggers were added in about 1450, after which they began to replace the longbow, as shown in this late 15th-century depiction of soldiers besieging a castle.

By the late 1300s, wrought-iron cannons could fire balls of 200–450 pounds (90–200 kg) and were making an impact on siege warfare. Then, in the 15th century, improved cast-bronze cannons made artillery more effective. For instance, when Charles VIII of France invaded Italy in 1494 and conducted a blitzkrieg through the north of the country, he used his cannons to reduce castles with amazing speed.

Nevertheless, mounted knights remained the most effective shock troops of medieval Europe up to the 15th century, when the use of gunpowder diminished their role. Part of the knight's effectiveness was due to his protective armor. Typical coverings included a padded undergarment; a chain-mail shirt, or hauberk, which often had a hood; a light overgarment, or surcoat; and an iron helmet. By the late 12th century, the helmet was usually pot- or barrel-shaped, with slits for the eyes and sometimes with a visor.

In the 1200s, plate armor began to be used. At first, it was fitted only over kneecaps, shins, and elbows; but in the course of the 15th century, it came to cover the whole body and could weigh up to 90 pounds (40 kg). Nor was it always entirely restrictive: a certain athletic French knight could execute a somersault fully clad in armor plates. A knight's weapons included an iron-tipped lance, 10 feet (3 m) long, which he used for his initial charge, and a sword, mace, or battle-ax, for use when dismounted. To supplement his armor, he carried a large kite-shaped shield typically made of wood, covered in hide, and bordered by a metal rim.

Apart from the longbow, the most effective weapons used to combat knights were crossbows, pikes, and halberds. The T-shaped crossbow fired a short heavy bolt and was usually primed by turning a crank against a ratchet. Although inferior to the longbow in range, accuracy, and rate of fire, it did not require the same muscle power or length of training. And its ability to pierce the armor of knights initially led to its being branded a barbaric weapon.

The pike and halberd were infantry weapons favored by Swiss soldiers. The pike – a metal-tipped staff up to 20 feet (6 m) long – was most lethal when used by dense clusters of soldiers. The halberd was a 6-foot (2-m) shaft topped by an ax with an upward-pointing blade for piercing armor and a backward-facing spike for hooking a knight off his mount. In 1315, fighting the troops of Duke Leopold of Austria, Swiss Eidgenossen, or "oath brothers," used halberds to destroy the cream of Leopold's cavalry.

In the 14th and 15th centuries, the increasing employment of gunpowder gradually affected the use of armor and hand weapons. Plate armor finally succumbed to harquebus and musket balls and, by the 16th century, was mainly ornamental. Firearms also eventually replaced the longbow and crossbow; the pike, however, was still important up to the end of the 17th century.

bIBLIOGRAPHY

The following is a
selection of volumes
used in the making
of this book, and
recommendations
for further reading.

Barber, Richard
*The Penguin Guide
to Medieval Europe*
Penguin Books,
London, 1984

Barlow, Frank
*The Feudal Kingdom of
England 1042–1216,*
Longman, London and
New York, 4th ed., 1988

Braunfels, Wolfgang
*Monasteries of Western
Europe* (trans. Alastair
Laing) Thames and
Hudson, London, 1972

Brooke, Christopher
*The Monastic World
1000–1300* Paul Elek
Ltd., London, 1974

Brown, R. Allen
Dover Castle English
Heritage, London, 3rd
ed., 1993

Brucker, Gene Adam
Florence 1138–1737
Sidgwick & Jackson,
London, 1984

Calkins, Robert G.
*Illuminated Books of the
Middle Ages* Thames and
Hudson, London, 1983

Colvin, H.M. (ed.)
*History of the King's
Works Vol. 2: The Middle
Ages* Her Majesty's
Stationery Office,
London, 1963

Conant, Kenneth John
*Carolingian and
Romanesque Architecture
800–1200* Penguin
Books, London,
2nd ed., 1966

——— "Medieval
Academy Excavations
at Cluny: Systematic
Dimensions of the
Buildings" in *Speculum*,
Cambridge,
Massachusetts, 1963

Davis, R.H.C,
*A History of Medieval
Europe* Longman,
Harlow, 1970

Dunan, Marcel (ed.)
*Larousse Encyclopedia of
Ancient and Medieval
History* (trans. Delano
Ames and Geoffrey
Sainsbury) Hamlyn,
Feltham, 1963

Evans, Joan (ed.) *The
Flowering of the Middle
Ages* Thames and
Hudson, London, 1985

Hallam, E.M. *Capetian
France, 987–1328*
Longman, Harlow,
1980

Hallam, E.M. (ed.)
*Chronicles of the Age of
Chivalry* Penguin
Books, London, 1987

——— *The Plantagenet
Chronicles* Penguin
Books, London, 1986

Hay, Denys
The Medieval Centuries
Methuen & Co. Ltd.,
London, 1964

Heer, Friedrich
*The Medieval World:
Europe 1100–1350*
Weidenfeld & Nicolson,
London, 1993

Hibbert, Christopher
*Florence: The Biography
of a City* Penguin Books,
London, 1993

Hindley, Geoffrey *The
Medieval Establishment*
Wayland, London, 1970

Holmes, George
The Oxford History of Medieval Europe
Oxford University Press, Oxford, 1988

Holmes, Richard
The World Atlas of Warfare Penguin Books, London, 1988

Hughes, Quentin
Military Architecture Hugh Evelyn, London, 1974

Keen, Maurice
The Pelican History of Medieval Europe Penguin Books, London, 1969

Knowles, David
Christian Monasticism Weidenfeld & Nicolson, London, 1969

Koenigsberger, H.G.
Medieval Europe 400–1500 Longman, Harlow, 1987

Lefroy, J.H.
"The Great Cannon of Muhammad II" in *The Archaeological Journal* Vol. 25, London, 1868

Longworth, Philip
The Making of Eastern Europe Macmillan, London and Basingstoke, 1992

Loyn, H.R. (ed.)
The Middle Ages: A Concise Encyclopaedia Thames and Hudson, London, 1989

Matthew, Donald
The Atlas of Medieval Europe Phaidon, Oxford, 1983

Neville, Peter
A Traveller's History of Russia and the USSR The Windrush Press, Gloucestershire, 1990

Panofsky, Erwin
Abbot Suger (ed. G. Panofsky-Soergel) Princeton University Press, New Jersey, 1979

Peters, Edward (ed.)
Heresy and Authority in Medieval Europe University of Pennsylvania, Philadelphia, 1980

Platt, Colin *The Atlas of Medieval Man* Macmillan, London and Basingstoke, 1979

———— *Dover Castle* English Heritage, London, 2nd ed., 1990

Sabietti, Mario and **Guido Alberto Rossi**
Florence from the Air (trans. J. Tyler Tuttle) Weidenfeld & Nicolson, London, 1989

Sayles, G.O. *The Medieval Foundations of England* Methuen & Co. Ltd., London, 1974

Seymour, William
Great Sieges of History Brassney's, London, 1991

Shaver-Crandell, Annie
The Cambridge Introduction to Art: The Middle Ages Cambridge University Press, Cambridge, 1982

Sherrard, Philip
Constantinople: Iconography of a Sacred City Oxford University Press, Oxford, 1965

Simons, Gerald
The Birth of Europe Time-Life Books, Virginia, 1980

Southern, R.W.
The Making of the Middle Ages Arrow Books, London, 1959

Toy, Sidney *A History of Fortification* William Heinemann Ltd., London, 1955

Waley, Daniel
The Italian City Republics World University Library/ Weidenfeld & Nicolson, London, 1969

———— *Later Medieval Europe* Longman, Harlow, 1964

Warner, Philip
Sieges of the Middle Ages G. Bell and Sons, Ltd., London, 1968

Wolff, Arnold
The Cologne Cathedral (trans. Margret Maranuk-Rohmeder) Vista Point Verlag, Cologne, 1990

Wood, Charles T.
The Age of Chivalry: Manners and Morals 1000–1450 Weidenfeld & Nicolson, London, 1970

INDEX

Page numbers in *italic* refer to illustrations and box text; those in **bold** denote gatefold spreads.

A

Aachen 11, *11*
abbeys *see* monasteries
abbots 19, 37, 83–84, *85*
Abd ar-Rahman I 22
Abelard, Peter 52, *53*
Acre 16, 38, 58, 97, 100
Agincourt, battle of 37, *110*, 111
Alaric *8*, 9
Albigensians (Cathars) 52, 94, *95*
Alcuin of York 11
Alexander III, Pope 16, *95*
Alexander V, Pope 79
Alexander VI, Pope 79
Alexander Nevsky, Prince *21*
Alexis, Saint, of Rome 94–95
Alexius I Comnenus, Emperor 99
Alfonso I the Magnanimous 17
Alfonso VI 22, *23*
Almohads 22
Almoravids 22, *23*
Ambrose, Saint *93*
Amiens 63, 64, *65*, 69
Andreas Capellanus 39
Angelico, Fra *61*
Angles *8*, 14
Anjou 14, 15, 110
Anselm of Laon 55
Anthony, Saint, of Egypt 82
Antioch (Turkey) 13, *98*, 100

Aquinas, Thomas, Saint 52
Aquitaine 14, 110, 111
Arabs (*see also* Muslims) *113*
archers *see* crossbows; longbows
Arezzo 45, *68*
Arians 9, *9*
Aristotle 22, 52, 93
armor 38, 97, 113, *113*
art 11, 66–68, *67*
Arthur, King 26, 38
Assisi *17*
Attila *8*
Augustine, Saint, of Canterbury 76
Augustine, Saint, of Hippo 52, 93, *94*
Averroës 22
Avignon 63, 78–79, *78*

B

"Babylonian Captivity" *78*, 79
Baghdad 13, 42
bailey 26, *26*, *31–33*
bailiffs 54, *55*
banking 17, 45, 58
barbican *31–33*
Bayeux Tapestry *26*
Beaumaris Castle 27
Beauvais 64
Becket, Thomas, Saint 14, *76*, 77
Benedict, Saint/Benedictines 81, 82, 83, 85, 92
Bernard of Chartres 52
Bernard of Clairvaux, Saint *53*, 61, 65, 66, *82–83*, 83–84, 92
Berry, Duc de *24*, *40*, *60–61*
bishops 19, 37
Black Death 16, 41, 55, 60–61, *60–61*

Black Prince [Edward] 109
Boabdil 23
Boccaccio, Giovanni 79
Bogolyubsky, Prince Andrey 21
Bologna 52, *53*
bolts 109, 113
Boniface VIII, Pope 78, *78*
books/manuscripts *10*, 11, 81, 92–93, *92–93*
Borgia, Rodrigo 79
Botticelli, Sandro *51*
Bouvines, battle of 15
Bruges 44, *54*, 58
Burgundy 111, *111*
Byzantium *see* Constantinople

C

Caernarfon Castle 27
Caesar, Julius 11, 45
Calais 111
Cambridge 52
cannons *see* gunpowder/guns
Canterbury *76*, 77, *77*, *93*
Capetians 14–15, 44
Carcassonne *42–43*, 95
Caroline minuscule *10*, 11, 92
Carolingians 10–11, *11*, 36, 45
Castel dell'Ova *26*
Castel del Monte 27
Castel Sant'Angelo *18*
castles 25–28, **29–35**, 97, 108, *109*, 113
Catania 27
catapults *see* weaponry; sieges
Cathars *see* Albigensians
cathedrals *12*, *13*, *17*, 52, 63–68, *64*, **69–75**
Cefalù *12*, *13*
Charlemagne, Emperor 9, 10–11, *10*, *11*, 18, 57, 69

Charles II of France *96*
Charles IV of France 111
Charles VII of France *37*, 111, *111*
Charles VIII of France *113*
Charles Martel 9
Chartres *12*, 52, 64, *66*, 68
Chateau Gaillard 25, 26–27, *27*
Chateau of Dourdan *24*
Chaucer, Geoffrey 38, 39, *77*
China *113*
chivalry 38
Christianity 8, 9, *9*, 10, 13, 20, 21, *21*
see also church; popes
church 18–19, *61*, 62–95
churches 11, *19–20*, *23*, *34–35*, 44, *44*, 55, 62, 63–68, *68*, *85*, 86, *90–91*
see also cathedrals
Cimabue *17*
Cistercians 66, 81, *82*, 83–84
Clare, Saint *84*
Clement V, Pope 78
Clement VII, Pope 79
Clermont, Council of 98
Clovis I, king of the Franks 9, *9*
Cluny/Cluniacs 83, **85–91**
Coca Castle *28*
Cologne 41, 42, 58, 63, **69–75**, *70–72*
Columbus, Christopher 23
condottieri 16
Constance, Council of 79
Constantine I the Great, Emperor 8–9, 69
Constantine XI, Emperor 102
Constantinople (Byzantium) 9, 10, 42, 45, 69, 102, *102*
culture *17*, 20, 27, 52, 64

Acknowledgments

Picture credits

l = left; *r* = right; *c* = center; *t* = top; *b* = bottom

Endpapers Charles Walker/Images; 2–3 Robert Harding Picture Library; 6 Bernard Cox/John Bethell; 7 Public Record Office; 9*t* Michael Holford, 9*b* AKG London; 10–11 *background image* British Museum/E.T. Archive, *main image* Angelo Hornak; 11 Musée Goya/Giraudon; 12 AKG London; 12–13 British Museum/AKG London; 13 Adam Woolfitt/Robert Harding Picture Library; 14*t* AKG London, 14*b* Bibliothèque Nationale/AKG London; 15*t* AKG London, 15*b* Joe Cornish; 16 AKG London; 17*l* John Heseltine, 17*r* AKG London; 18*t* AKG London, 18*b* John Bethell; 19 AKG London; 20 Irene Lynch/Impact; 21 AKG London; 22 Musée Conde/Giraudon/Bridgeman Art Library; 23*l* Michael Busselle, 23*r* Joe Cornish; 24 Musée Conde/Giraudon/Bridgeman Art Library; 26*t* Michael Holford/Musée de Bayeux, 26*b* Angelo Hornak; 27 Michael Holford; 28 Michael Busselle; **Gatefold: 29, 30 & 35, 34** *both* English Heritage Photographic Library; 36 Public Record Office; 36–7 President and Fellows of Corpus Christi College Oxford/John Gibbons; 37 Bibliothèque de Toulouse/Bridgeman Art Library; 38*t* Victoria & Albert Museum/E.T. Archive, 38*b* Biblioteca Marciana/E.T. Archive; 39*t* British Library/E.T. Archive, 39*b* Bibliothèque Nationale/Bridgeman Art Library; 40 Musée Conde/Giraudon/Bridgeman Art Library; 42–3 Images; 43 Ecole des Beaux Arts/Giraudon/Bridgeman Art Library; 44 Joe Cornish; **Gatefold: 45** Joe Cornish/Tony Stone Worldwide, 46 & 51 Joe Cornish, 50*t* Scala, 50*c* K & B News Foto/Bridgeman Art Library, 50*b* Scala; 52 Joe Cornish; 53*t* Musée Conde/Giraudon/Bridgeman Art Library, 53*b* Museo Civico/Scala; 54 Bibliothèque Nationale/Bridgeman Art Library; 55 E.T. Archive; 56 Victoria & Albert Museum/Bridgeman Art Library; 57*l* Fitzwilliam Museum, University of Cambridge/Bridgeman Art Library, 57*r* British Library/Bridgeman Art Library; 59*t* Staatsarchiv, Hamburg/Bridgeman Art Library, 59*b* Bibliothèque Nationale/Bridgeman Art Library; 60 Österreichische Nationalbibliothek/Bridgeman Art Library; 60–1 Musée Conde/Giraudon/Bridgeman Art Library; 61 Museo di San Marco dell'Angelico/Bridgeman Art Library; 62 Avila Cathedral/Index/Bridgeman Art Library; 64*t* Bernard Cox/John Bethell, 64*b* Bibliothèque Nationale/Bridgeman Art Library; 65 Roger Moss; 66 Joe Cornish; 66–7 Erich Lessing/AKG London; 68*t* Joe Cornish, 68*b* AKG London; **Gatefold: 69** Kinne/Zefa, 70 & 75 Angelo Hornak, 74 *both* Erich Lessing/AKG London; 77*l* Joe Cornish, 77*r* British Library/E.T. Archive; 78 British Library/Bridgeman Art Library; 78–9 Joe Cornish; 79 AKG London; 80 Christie's Images; 82 Joe Cornish; 82–3 John Bethell; 83 Michael Busselle; 84*t* Caroline Penn/Impact, 84*b* Louvre/Giraudon/Bridgeman Art Library; **Gatefold: 85** Joe Cornish; 86 & 91 Bernard Beaujard, 90*t* Bibliothèque Nationale, 90*c* Jason Wood, 90*b* Ministère de la Défense, Service Historique de l'Armée de Terre/Giraudon; 92 Miki Slingsby/Dean and Chapter of Winchester Cathedral; 93*t* Christie's Images, 93*c* Trinity College, Cambridge/Bridgeman Art Library, 93*b* Christie's Images; 94 Prado, Madrid/Bridgeman Art Library; 95 British Library/Bridgeman Art Library; 96 Christie's Images; 98 E.T. Archive; 99 *both* Bibliothèque Nationale/Bridgeman Art Library; 100 *both* British Library/Bridgeman Art Library; **Gatefold: 101** Board of Trustees of the Royal Armouries, 102 & 107 Samih Rifat, 106*t* National Gallery, 106*b* Bernard Cox/John Bethell; 108 Bibliothèque Municipale de Lyon/Bridgeman Art Library; 109 British Library/Bridgeman Art Library; 110 Bibliothèque Nationale/Bridgeman Art Library; 111 Archives Nationales/Giraudon/Bridgeman Art Library; 112 Bibliothèque Nationale/Bridgeman Art Library; 113–14 British Library/Bridgeman Art Library; 116–120 Christie's Images.

Artwork credits

Ivan Lapper: gatefolds 31–4, 47–50, 71–4, 87–90, 103–6
Lorraine Harrison: ground plans and maps 8–9, 31, 47, 58–9, 71, 76–7, 87, 103
John Hutchinson: borders and chapter identification icons
Gary Cross 106*r*

Marshall Editions would like to thank Louise Tucker, Ken Scott, and John Iveson, as well as the following for their assistance in the compilation of this book:
Copy editors Isabella Raeburn, Maggi McCormick
Managing editor Lindsay McTeague
Editorial director Sophie Collins
DTP editors Mary Pickles, Pennie Jelliff
Indexer Judy Batchelor
Production Sarah Hinks
Production editor Sorrel Everton